THE CHALLENGE OF DRUG TRAFFICKING TO DEMOCRATIC GOVERNANCE AND HUMAN SECURITY IN WEST AFRICA

INTRODUCTION: BROAD CONTEXT OF DRUG TRAFFICKING IN WEST AFRICA

West Africa is under attack from international criminal networks that are using the subregion as a key global hub for the distribution, wholesale, and increasing production of illicit drugs.[1] Most of the drug trade in West Africa involves cocaine sold in Europe, although heroin is also trafficked to the United States; the subregion is becoming an export base for amphetamines and their precursors, mainly for East Asian markets and increasingly to the United States.[2] At least nine top-tier Latin American drug cartels have already established bases in at least 11 of 16 West African nations.[3] Their illicit profits threaten U.S. national security interests by strengthening criminal elements in Latin America that also traffic drugs to North America. For example, the same Latin drug trafficking organizations (DTOs) transporting cocaine via West Africa to Europe are also responsible for cocaine shipments via Mexico to the United States. Responding to this, the U.S. Drug Enforcement Agency (DEA) has revised its counternarcotics strategy and is carrying out investigative efforts against these DTOs on both sides of the Atlantic Ocean.[4]

In recent years, West Africa has grown exponentially from a minor trafficking route for cocaine exports to a major hub.[5] It was not until 2004 that large-scale cocaine trafficking through West Africa was first detected. Prior to this, annual cocaine seizure levels in West Africa had rarely exceeded one

1

metric ton per year. Already by 2008, cocaine transshipments rivaled stolen crude oil for the most valuable smuggled commodity in West Africa.[6] Estimates of 2010 annual cocaine transshipments through West Africa ranged widely between 46 and 300 tons, yielding wholesale revenues of $3 billion to $14 billion. By some measures, 50 percent of non-U.S.-bound cocaine now goes through West Africa, i.e., about 13 percent of global flows.[7] African authorities actually detected fewer drugs in 2010 than in the 2 prior years, but this is likely because traffickers switched to new conveyances and routes.[8] The hiding of drugs in containers on commercial vessels, for example, is a new strategy whose use probably expanded. In July 2010, a container with 450 kilos of cocaine was seized in Lagos, Nigeria, on a vessel arriving from Chile. In January 2011, two other vessels seized in Nigeria had a total of 275 kilos of cocaine,[9] one of which contained 110 kilos arriving from Bolivia.[10] Another tactic was to route an increasing number of containers through Argentina and Uruguay toward West Africa.[11] In November 2012, authorities in Guyana seized 350 kilos of cocaine hidden in a shipping container filled with soap powder destined for Nigeria.[12]

West Africa's emergence as a trafficking nexus was also symptomatic of a shift in the center of gravity of the global market for cocaine from the United States to Europe. This shift occurred due to structural factors including a declining and saturated U.S. cocaine market, heightened European demand for cocaine, the stronger euro making sales of this drug more lucrative in Europe,[13] the existence of well-developed West African smuggling networks as ready-made partners,[14] and successful interdiction efforts including anti-money laundering measures[15] that drove drug traffickers away from traditional trafficking routes into North America and Europe, including via the Caribbean and Spain.[16]

West Africa's geographical location between Latin America and Europe made it an ideal transit zone for exploitation by powerful drug cartels and terrorist organizations. In this sense, many West African countries are now suffering the adverse effects of the geographic accident of lying between the sites of drug production and the most lucrative consumption markets—much as the Caribbean and Central America had long suffered from being placed between South America's cocaine producers and North America's cocaine users.[17] Dakar, Senegal, for example, is roughly a midway point between Latin America and Europe, and is actually 700 miles closer to Recife, Brazil, than it is to Paris, France.

West Africa's primary operational allure to traffickers is not actually geography, however, but rather its low standards of governance, low levels of law enforcement capacity, and high rates of corruption.[18] Traffickers gain competitive advantages by operating in West African states with the weakest rule of law.[19] Powerful cartels and terrorist organizations both thrive in West Africa's permissive environment and its vast ungoverned sea, land, and air spaces.[20] West Africa's borders—including its maritime domain—are largely unguarded. The region boasts more than 2,600 miles of coastline. To put things in perspective, the U.S. Pacific coast (minus Alaska) and Atlantic coast each are less than 2,100 miles long.[21] Then United Nations Office on Drugs and Crime (UNODC) Executive Director Antonio Maria Costa accurately captured West Africa's dilemma when he summarized its drug trafficking situation in 2008:

Drug planes don't have to fly below the radar, because in most cases there is no radar (or electricity). Soldiers sometimes help smugglers by closing airports and unloading the cargo. Police cars run out of gas when giving chase or are left in the dust by smugglers' all-terrain vehicles. There are no local navies to intercept ships coming from Latin America or to chase 2,000-horespower boats that speed drugs up the coast to Europe. Traffickers are seldom brought to trial; in some cases, there are no prisons to put them in. Even when they are charged they are usually released because evidence is not collected or needed laws are not in place.[22]

West Africa's governance, law enforcement, and corruption challenges are linked to the subregion's underdevelopment. All but three of 16 nations in West Africa are on the United Nations (UN) list of "least developed countries," including the five countries with the very lowest levels of human development.[23] Ten of the top 41 countries in the "2012 Failed States Index" were in West Africa (and 25 of the top 41 were in sub-Saharan Africa).[24] Current UNODC Executive Director Yuri Fedotov framed the linkage between underdevelopment in the subregion and transnational crime in February 2012 as follows:

South American drug cartels are exploiting regional vulnerabilities in West Africa: poverty, unemployment, lack of border control, weakness of law enforcement structures, and endemic corruption. . . . For these criminals, West Africa represents not only the shortest, but also the most cost-effective channel for trafficking illicit drugs to Europe.[25]

Deputy Assistant Secretary of Defense for Counternarcotics and Global Threats William Wechsler

4

recently characterized the challenges faced by the subregion as follows:

> West Africa is now facing a situation analogous to the Caribbean in the 1980s, where small, developing, vulnerable countries along major drug-trafficking routes toward rich consumers are vastly under-resourced to deal with the wave of dirty money coming their way.[26]

HISTORY OF DRUG TRAFFICKING IN WEST AFRICA

Drug trafficking is not a new phenomenon in West Africa, but consideration of this history is important to illuminate the entrenched nature of the drug trade in the subregion, and its negative implications for democratic development.[27] The historical reality is that trade routes for illicit (and licit) goods have existed for hundreds of years in West Africa and are ensconced in local traditions, especially in the Sahelo-Saharan region.[28] Consistent with this, the pre-independence economies of West Africa were characterized by a variety of illicit, shadow economies. Cannabis trafficking in West Africa was documented almost a century ago, in the 1920s, and is still widespread today. Annual cannabis production in West Africa is about 3,500 tons/year.[29] There were seizures in September 2011 and February 2012 of five and one tons respectively of cannabis resin being transported to Europe via northern Niger in Toyota 4X4s.[30] The first documented use of West Africa as a staging post for international heroin smuggling dates from 1952, when U.S. officials noted that parcels of the drug were being transported by a Lebanese syndicate from Beirut to New York via Kano, Nigeria, and Accra, Ghana.[31] While cocaine trafficking has become a recent focal point of international attention on West Africa, the subregion actually has a long history of trafficking and organized crime.[32] West Africa received less notoriety, however, only because the subregion, and indeed all of sub-Saharan Africa, generally played only a peripheral role in global drug trafficking prior to the mid-2000s.[33]

Generally speaking, the roots of West Africa's transformation into a major international trade hub in illegal drugs may be traced to the 1960s. It was then that the first reports emerged of locally grown cannabis being exported from Nigeria to Europe in significant quantities.[34] By the 1970s, Ghanaian smugglers had joined Nigerians in exporting African-grown cannabis to Europe on a scale large enough to attract sustained official attention. Starting from the 1980s, production, distribution, and consumption of cannabis provided pathways for the incorporation of heroin and cocaine into West Africa's drug trade. At that time, Nigerian smugglers started sending heroin by air courier from Pakistan to Nigeria, where it was repackaged and re-exported to the United States.[35] By the 1990s, Ghana became an early transit point for the international cocaine trade, and in Accra it was public knowledge which houses were built by cocaine money, and which flashy cars were cocaine cars.[36] Nigeria still plays a huge role in the international heroin trade, with intercepted stocks amounting to about 70 kilograms (kg) seized in the country per year.[37] Besides Nigerian and Ghanaian global networks, major new ones have developed involving Côte d'Ivoire and Senegal nationals.[38]

By the 1990s, Nigerian drug traders had largely finished the process of "internationalizing" their business. Nigerian drug traffickers had not only developed the means to make bulk shipments of narcotics, but had also become fully global, having a "headquarters" (home) country, business associates in both producing and consuming countries, and facilities in countries outside Nigeria.[39] Part of the reason that Nigerian drug traffickers have been so successful is that their home country has provided them with a relatively permissive environment. Perhaps the most important local partner of Nigerian drug traders in the 1990s was the Nigerian military, which by then had developed a high degree of impunity after being in power almost continuously for many years.[40]

Within West Africa, Nigerians established operational centers in Cotonou, Benin, and Abidjan, Cote d'Ivoire.[41] Outside the continent, they established sales networks in major U.S., European and post-Soviet Union cities, including Geneva, Switzerland,[42] where they are active in cocaine trafficking, and Moscow, Russia, where they took over heroin retailing.[43] In Asia, there are large networks of Nigerian air couriers, some bringing heroin transiting or stopping in West Africa, and others transporting cocaine and methamphetamines, ecstasy, and ketamine from West Africa toward Asia (and Australia); these often transit via Malaysia or Indonesia, to Japan, Korea, China, Thailand, and Singapore.[44] Since 2009, Nigerian and Ghanaian DTOs diversified into trafficking crystalline methamphetamine through links with other West African countries such as Benin, Cote d'Ivoire, Guinea, and Senegal.[45]

LATIN AMERICAN DRUG DEALERS PARTNER WITH WEST AFRICAN CRIMINALS

One typical way that the Latin American drug cartels operate is to send lieutenants to open legitimate businesses in West African nations in order to obtain their legal residency papers, and start the process of setting up local illegal networks and front companies to facilitate drug trafficking.[46] Once installed, the Latin Americans partner with transnational organized crime (TOC) groups in West Africa, particularly Nigerians, for their smuggling and trafficking expertise, safe houses, storage space, banking, and a host of other services.[47] This is analogous to how Colombian cartels established links with Mexican syndicates after the United States significantly choked off the old Caribbean drug transportation corridor and forced the Colombians to start moving their drug loads across the southwest border of the United States.[48] Mexican DTOs, including the Sinaloa cartel, are also present in West Africa.[49] There have also been reports of Venezuelans, Surinamese, and European organizations including Italian TOCs operating in the same territory.[50]

The degree to which Latin American traffickers rely on West African partners, and the nature of these partnerships, depend heavily on the quality of law enforcement in each African country. In countries such as Guinea-Bissau, which has extremely weak governance, Latin American cartels need only bribe the only institution with real power — the military — and are then able to enjoy de facto freedom from prosecution. In other countries, such as Ghana, which has an emerging democratic tradition and stronger state institutions, Latin American cartels rely more on local partners, thus insulating themselves from possible arrest by local authorities. Not surprisingly, while law enforcement authorities continue to arrest low-level narcotics traffickers, Ghana has had relatively limited success in pursuing Latin American partners and their Ghanaian drug baron partners.[51]

STRUCTURE OF WEST AFRICAN DTOS

The general structure of most West African criminal networks has distinctive characteristics typical of lineage-based societies.[52] Criminal enterprises in West Africa use similar techniques to those of legitimate traders and business people: A successful individual entrepreneur invites one or more junior relatives or dependents to join him or her in a business deal.[53] West African criminal networks, in general, have certain prime characteristics, including:

- Small, compartmentalized cells of between two and 10 members;
- Mostly kinsmen from the same ethnic group or tribe;
- The ability to communicate mostly in indigenous, African languages;
- Making deals and then dispersing, regrouping at a later date as needed;
- Adopting false identities for its members, including changing their nationality; and,
- Refraining from the use of violence in order not to attract the attention of law enforcement officials.[54]

Some observers have juxtaposed so-called "horizontally" structured African criminal gangs with the so-called "vertically" structured Latin American cartels. This is a flawed analogy, however, as West African societies remain relatively traditional and hierarchical. The West African modus operandi closely resembles an "adhocracy," which is able to fuse experts drawn from different disciplines into smoothly functioning, yet, ad hoc project teams.[55] This stands in

9

contrast to the more corporate-style relations of classic American mafias. Moreover, "informal" or "ad hoc" is not intended to imply that West African traffickers are not capable. A senior U.S. anti-drug official once described Nigerian drug networks as "some of the most sophisticated and finely-tuned transshipment, money–moving and document-forging organizations in the world."[56] West African trafficking groups have shown a high degree of flexibility in their amphetamine-type stimulants (ATS) trafficking routes by using couriers from countries outside the region, e.g., from Eastern Europe or Asia, and by diversifying their routes, which are mostly by air.[57]

Nigerian drug traffickers are also "decentralized and diversified" into TOC lines of business, including "illicit drugs, prostitution, and scams."[58] Consistent with this, Nigerians dominate the markets for cocaine and prostitution in Rome, Milan, Naples, Genoa, and other Italian cities, in collaboration with the Calabrese and Camorra mafia,[59] and may be more accurately considered to be TOC members than merely DTOs. This being said, most indigenous organized crime groups in West Africa, with the Nigerians and Ghanaians being exceptions, have historically lacked the sophistication of global drug trafficking cartels. Unfortunately, West Africans are catching up by partnering and learning from the Latin American drug cartels.[60]

GLOBAL DRUG TRAFFICKING ROUTES VIA WEST AFRICA

Global drug trafficking routes that pass through or originate in West Africa vary by the type of drug involved:

1. **Heroin.** This drug is principally smuggled by West African criminal groups from Afghanistan and

Pakistan, through Iran and other Middle Eastern countries, on to East or Southern Africa, then to West Africa before being transported to the United States and Europe. Nigeria and Ghana are the principal transit zones in West Africa, with Cote d'Ivoire another key transit country.[61] By contrast, heroin coming from South America, especially Colombia, often traverses the Atlantic to West Africa, only to cross back to North American markets.[62] In both routes, heroin is transported from the source zone by a variety of means, including maritime containers, go-fast boats, small wooden fishing vessels called *dhows*, air drops at sea, air cargo, and luggage and body-carried by couriers or "mules."[63]

Nigerian nationals accounted for 32 percent of drug trafficking arrests in Pakistan from 2000-08, with Ghanaian, Guineans, and Ivoirians accounting for 1 percent each.[64] During July 2011, the DEA Office in Accra, in coordination with the Ghana Sensitive Investigative Unit (SIU), concluded an investigation targeting a Ghana-based organization responsible for shipping multikilogram quantities of heroin from West Africa to the United States. That month, U.S. federal agents took down an international heroin-trafficking ring that moved heroin from Ghana to Dulles International Airport outside of Washington, DC.[65]

Smaller countries in West Africa are also touched by the international heroin trade. In May 2011, the DEA Office in Lagos, Nigeria, in coordination with DEA Islamabad and the Benin judicial police, interdicted 200 kgs of heroin from Pakistan that was in transit in Cotonou, Benin. This undercover operation resulted in the single largest heroin seizure in Benin's history, and the arrest of three Beninese and one Togolese in Benin and several arrests in Pakistan.[66]

2. **Methamphetamine.** Illicit manufacture of methamphetamine is not entirely new to the African continent. Since 2004, regular reports of illicit manufacture of the substance have been received from South Africa.[67] Since 2007, the DEA has assisted with the seizure of several other multiton pseudoephedrine and ephedrine shipments in Africa that have been linked to Mexican DTOs[68] in Nigeria, Ghana, Kenya, the Democratic Republic of the Congo (DRC), and Mozambique.[69] Mexican cartels are gaining a foothold in West Africa, where their traffickers are being used as advisors and possibly being recruited as chemists in the illicit manufacture of methamphetamine.[70]

West Africa has been a transshipment area for precursor chemicals diverted for methamphetamine production since at least 2009, with large increases in shipments through Benin, Cote d'Ivoire, and Senegal,[71] and with Nigeria and Ghana as likely production hubs based on increased precursor shipments. The added danger with ATS is that, unlike cocaine and heroin, illicit ATS manufacture does not rely on the cultivation of naturally occurring plants such as the coca leaf or opium poppy and, as such, is not limited to certain geographic locations—leaving the possibility that West Africa could be transformed not only into a key transit point for ATS, but into a manufacturing hub as well.[72] The DEA has already documented the emergence of West Africa as a significant production point of origin for multikilogram methamphetamine shipments to the Far East.

Evidence was uncovered in July 2009 of intended ATS manufacture in Guinea, with precursor chemicals sufficient to manufacture ecstasy worth over $100 million.[73] In April 2010, 36 kilos of crystal methamphetamine destined for Japan and five kilos of methamphetamine destined for the United States via South Africa were seized on cargo planes in Nigeria.[74] In June 2010, Cote d'Ivoire officials seized precursor chemicals acetone destined for Benin and methyl ethyl ketone destined for Guinea.[75] In 2010, the International Narcotics Control Board reportedly stopped shipments of 500 kg and 200 kg of ephedrine headed for Guinea and Niger.[76] In 2010, the United States Government indicted members of a large international cocaine trafficking organization for, *inter alia,* the intent to establish a clandestine laboratory in Liberia for the large-scale manufacture of methamphetamine that would have been destined for Japan and the United States.[77]

Because of limited reporting to UNODC by West African countries, the best measure of the escalating situation appears to be reports coming from countries in East and Southeast Asia of the increasing involvement of West African nationals. While China and Taiwan have traditionally been the source countries for methamphetamine smuggled into Japan, the proportion of seized methamphetamine trafficked into Japan from Africa rose from 7.4 percent in 2009 to 36 percent in the first half of 2010, mostly from Nigeria.[78]

The most common destinations for methamphetamine trafficked through Africa have been Japan, followed by Korea. Since March 2010, numerous arrests of couriers in Asia attempting to smuggle methamphetamine from Africa indicates African drug syndicates produce the drug for export throughout the Asia-Pacific region, with most of the Africa-sourced methamphetamine destined for sale in Japan following transshipment through countries such as Malaysia[79] and Thailand.[80] In May 2011, there were two seizures in Nigeria of 63 kilos of methamphetamines and 26 kilos of amphetamines destined for Japan, and a seizure in Senegal of one kilo of methamphetamine from a courier from Togo heading to Japan. According to a European police official based in Africa, Nigerian criminal networks were building links to Japan's yakuza criminal gangs.[81]

French anti-drug officials agree that most methamphetamine production in West Africa is destined for East and Southeast Asia, including also China, Cambodia, Vietnam, and the Philippines.[82] Since 2010, West African groups, particularly Nigerians, have trafficked methamphetamine to New Zealand[83] and likely Australia as well.

In 2011, the DEA and Nigeria's drug enforcement agency jointly initiated two additional investigations targeting clandestine methamphetamine operators either based in Nigeria or selling their labs' illicit production in Nigeria. These operators are actively seeking organized criminal group assistance in legally importing and then diverting large-scale quantities of precursor chemicals into Nigeria to increase their methamphetamine production capacity.[84] An operating methamphetamine laboratory was discovered in Lagos, Nigeria, in June 2011, which was estimated to be capable of producing 150-200 kgs per week.[85] A second operational lab was seized in February 2012, and one Nigerian and three Bolivians arrested — suggesting possible cooperation with Latin American criminal syndicates.[86]

Togo's Security and Protection Minister was quoted in August 2012 as saying that the drug trafficking situation in West Africa has reached "worrying proportions . . . especially after the illegal setting up of laboratories to manufacture amphetamine drugs in the subregion."[87] While West Africa is not currently an important source region for the importation of methamphetamine drugs into the United States, it may become so in the future. As Senator Dianne Feinstein pointed out during a Senate hearing that she chaired in May 2012:

> Methamphetamine and other illegal drugs produced in Africa could very well make their way to U.S. markets one day. Some methamphetamine currently produced in Africa is being shipped all the way to Southeast Asia. There is no reason to believe that methamphetamine produced in Africa could not make it into the United States in the future.[88]

Senator Feinstein's concerns are well placed. Most countries in West Africa do not have the legislative and institutional frameworks necessary to control precursor trafficking. As has been the case with heroin and cocaine, traffickers are taking advantage of the subregion's permissive environment to import chemical precursors and, increasingly, use these locally in the illicit manufacturing of ATS drugs.[89]

3. **Cocaine.** Colombia produces about 54 percent of the refined cocaine on the world market, with the rest coming from Bolivia and Peru.[90] Prior to about 2004, cocaine destined for Europe had followed a northerly route from South America, through the eastern Caribbean to Spain's Canary Islands and Portugal's Azores Islands, to clandestine landing zones on the coast of Spain, Portugal, and the Netherlands or to commercial ports such as Barcelona, Rotterdam, and Antwerp.[91] Besides Spain, Portugal, and the Netherlands, other major European entry points for cocaine included France and Italy.[92]

However, heightened U.S. anti-drug and counter-terrorism law enforcement and border control efforts, coupled with U.S. and European interdiction, forced smuggling further south to destinations in West Africa from Mauritania to as far south and east as Nigeria.[93] Around 2004, West Africans began to provide logistical assistance to South American cocaine traffickers in organizing their West African maritime shipments to Europe from at least two subregions: one centered on Guinea-Bissau and Guinea in the western Gulf of Guinea, and the other centered on the Bight of Benin, including Ghana, Togo, Benin, and Nigeria.[94] This first subregion was along Latitude 10 North between northern South America and the western part of Africa's coast, and became so important that law enforcement agencies dubbed it "Highway 10."[95] Europol has recently confirmed that former hashish-smuggling routes are also being used by cocaine traffickers.[96] These routes may involve Moroccan nationals who have gained smuggling expertise through years of trafficking hashish across the Mediterranean.[97] Algeria is also an important hub for drugs of all kinds, with numerous reports of the arrests of couriers.[98]

In 2007, U.S. and international authorities estimated that approximately 80 percent of cocaine traveling from Latin America to Africa moved by sea and 20 percent by air.[99] There may be as many as 100 ships that cross the Atlantic every year transporting drugs to West Africa.[100] Anecdotal evidence suggests cartels have even used submarines.[101] The largest known loads of cocaine en route to Europe via West Africa have been transported by large commercial fishing or freight "mother ships" that hand off shipments to smaller, faster boats outside territorial waters (including fishing boats, sailing yachts, and speedboats).[102]

According to Europol, the crews of these smaller vessels are often West African, with Spanish or South American "controllers."[103]

In addition to ships, about 60 illicit aircraft regularly make the cross-Atlantic journey, benefiting from an abundance of landing strips and limited air traffic control.[104] After arriving in West Africa, the cocaine is transported in small quantities by couriers on commercial flights, and sometimes by air freight or by smugglers across the Sahara to North Africa and then Europe.[105] A 2008 Department of Homeland Security report warned of a growing fleet of rogue aircraft crisscrossing the Atlantic—at least 10 aircraft, including executive jets, twin-engine turboprops, and aging Boeing 727s.[106] UNODC reported in 2010 that a number of modified aircraft had taken off from Venezuela toward West Africa, "notably to Cape Verde, Guinea-Bissau, Mali, Mauritania, and Sierra Leone."[107] Some smaller aircraft are modified for the transatlantic voyage by the inclusion of additional fuel tanks.[108] Some airports or landing strips are also in the Sahara-Sahel.[109] In November 2009, a burned Boeing 727 was found in the desert of northern Mali after having served to transport several tons of cocaine on a flight from Venezuela.[110] One affluent area of Gao, in northeastern Mali, had been known as "Cocainebougou"— at least until the March 2012 Al-Qaeda in the Islamic Maghreb (AQIM)/Touareg takeover of that city. [111]

Much of Colombia's cocaine exports to Europe are now passing through Venezuela and Brazil and then transiting through West Africa via air and ship. A significant portion of the Bolivian (and, to a lesser degree, Peruvian) cocaine shipments are also moving by air via Venezuela, in part because of the "Bolivarian Revolutionary" alliance between Bolivian President Evo Morales, himself a coca farmer before rising to power, and Venezuelan President Hugo Chávez.[112] Several of the largest cocaine busts in West Africa have come aboard aircraft that departed from Venezuela.[113] The majority of the Bolivian and Peruvian cocaine is moved through Brazil and then onward to Africa. There are linguistic as well as geographic reasons for the Brazil connection. Guinea-Bissau, and Cape Verde, two of the most active transshipment hubs, are former Portuguese colonies, like Brazil.[114] This Brazil connection was facilitated by increased air transport links between Brazil and Africa. Consistent with this, in November 2011, there were two seizures at the Lagos, Nigeria, airport from passengers on a Qatar Airlines flight from Sao Paulo, Brazil.[115] Brazil is now rivaling Venezuela as the number one point of departure for cocaine transported to Africa.

Wholesale Distribution and Sale Shifts to West Africa.

In recent years, Latin American traffickers also relocated a share of their wholesale distribution from the Western Hemisphere to West Africa. This means that the subregion has moved from being merely a short-term transit point to becoming a storage and staging area for wholesale repackaging, re-routing, and sometimes (re-)sale of drugs.[116] It also means, as Antonio Mazzitelli, UNODC regional representative for West and Central Africa, put it, that "West Africa is changing more and more from being just a stockpiling place into a hub where cocaine is traded."[117]

Recent UNODC drug seizure data of stockpiled cocaine suggest that multiple subregional repackaging and redistribution trafficking patterns have emerged in the Economic Community of West African States's (ECOWAS's) 15 member-states, as well as Mauritania and Morocco. In recent years, there were confirmed cases of traffickers who stockpiled cocaine in Nigeria, Benin, Togo, Ghana, Guinea, Guinea-Bissau, Senegal, Cape Verde, and Mauritania. One route involves cocaine entering Guinea-Bissau that is then routed to Senegal, Guinea, Gambia, and Mali for onward transport to Europe.[118] Leopold Senghor International Airport in Dakar is known to be a crucial departure point in West Africa en route to Europe. Bamako's international airport has become another important transit point for drug traffickers, especially Nigerians, transporting drugs to Europe.[119] Another route involves Cape Verde, where in October 2011 the DEA worked with local and Dutch authorities to make the largest recorded cocaine seizure in that country's history.[120]

One academic, citing news reports, has written that:

> Nigerian middlemen have also played a leading role in the development of a trans–Saharan route for smuggling cocaine into Europe, sometimes using Touareg guides. In early 2008, Malian authorities seized 750 kilos of cocaine at Tinzawatine in the middle of the Sahara. . . . Once cocaine reaches North Africa, established Moroccan hashish smugglers can take it to Europe.[121]

In June 2011, French law enforcement separately assisted in the seizure of 400 kgs of cocaine destined for Niger.[122]

Latin American groups are employing West Africans to handle cocaine shipments in West Africa, paying for these services in cocaine. This has led to two parallel systems of importation to Europe: one involving larger quantities remaining under South American control, and one involving smaller quantities owned by West Africans. The former is more likely to use maritime shipments, while the latter more often uses couriers on commercial air flights, a favored technique of West African groups worldwide.[123] A typical West African air courier tactic is the so-called "shotgun approach," in which as many as 30 couriers are placed on board a single flight with the knowledge that customs officers only have the capacity to arrest and process a limited number of them. Some traffickers will put couriers on a single commercial flight from places like Accra, Ghana, to the European Union (EU), and will then give the name of one courier to the authorities on the receiving end to focus law enforcement on that individual, allowing the remainder to proceed unchecked.[124] Finally, the wider availability of cocaine at the wholesale level and the consequent development of a regional market have generated a new group of operators, the "freelancers." These people, often Europeans or West Africans with valid resident permits in Europe, invest their savings in the purchase of a couple of kilos of cocaine with the objective of smuggling it to Europe.[125]

LINK TO TERRORISM: ALLIANCES BETWEEN DRUG TRAFFICKERS AND TERRORISTS

Criminal enterprises are evolving into new hybrid organizations that blur the traditional distinction between organized crime and terrorism.[126] There is evidence that some of these hybrid organizations have ties to West Africa. Both groups exploit the same state weaknesses and are increasingly overlapping in using the same "shadow facilitators," or criminal specialists, for money laundering, weapons trafficking, human trafficking, smuggling, document forgery, transportation, security, and strategic corruption.[127]

These growing links in West Africa between drug trafficking, other forms of transnational organized crime, and international terrorism represent a new security threat to the United States. Consistent with this, President Obama's *Strategy to Combat Transnational Organized Crime*, released in July 2011, declared organized crime to be a national security threat, and was a significant step forward in addressing this "crime-terror-insurgency nexus."[128] Four terrorist groups or state sponsors of terrorism active in drug trafficking in West Africa are:

1. **Revolutionary Armed Forces of Colombia (FARC).** There are precedents in other regions of the world for terrorists using the drug trade to finance their activities. In 2010, 18 of 44 international terrorist groups designated by the United States had been linked to some aspect of the international drug trade.[129] Through much of the 1990s and 2000s, the FARC funded its insurgency in Colombia through cocaine production and kidnapping.[130] President Chávez in Venezuela has allowed the FARC, with whom many observers believe he has a deep and personal relationship, to establish routes through his country that greatly lessen the threat and the cost of moving cocaine.[131] Some of the cocaine-smuggling operations in West Africa have been linked to the FARC, including an April 2007 arrest and subsequent unexplained release in Guinea-Bissau of two FARC officials in connection with the discovery of a large consignment of cocaine.[132] In May 2010, an investigation targeting two DTOs revealed that six tons of cocaine purchased from the FARC were transported on a plane originating in Venezuela and transited Liberia for eventual

21

distribution into Europe and the United States.[133] This successful investigation was made possible by the cooperation of Liberian officials, including the Director of National Security, who is the son of President Sirleaf Johnson.[134]

2. **Al-Qaeda in the Islamic Maghreb (AQIM).** Other international terrorist groups already present in West Africa are also increasingly engaging in drug trafficking to finance their activities, including the likely purchase of sophisticated weaponry. According to UN Secretary General Ban Ki-Moon, an assessment mission dispatched in December 2011 to look at the effects of the Libya crisis on the Sahel found that terrorist groups such as AQIM had begun to form alliances with drug traffickers and other criminal syndicates.[135] The link to AQIM takes on particular significance in light of this terrorist organization's March 2012 takeover of northern Mali, along with the AQIM splinter group Movement for Unity and Jihad in West Africa (MUJAO) and Touareg allies such as Ansar Dine.[136]

In December 2009, the DEA's Ghanaian counterparts arrested three suspected members and facilitators of AQIM based upon a United States arrest warrant stemming from a narco-terrorism indictment in the Southern District of New York. The charges in this case marked the first time that associates of al-Qaeda had been charged with narco-terrorism offenses. All three defendants pleaded guilty.[137] AQIM has profited from North Africa's drug smuggling and West Africa's assorted smuggling enterprises, such as in Mali and Western Sahara.[138] AQIM collects a "tax" on traffickers who pass through territory under its control.[139] Touareg rebels in the north of Mali and Niger have also been involved in trans-Saharan trafficking.[140]

3. **Hezbollah.** Given the prominence of the Lebanese diaspora community in West Africa and its members' control of pipelines to import and export illegal commodities, it was inevitable that those organizations and the drug trafficking groups would link up.[141] A U.S. investigation codenamed Operation TITAN unraveled a Lebanese-dominated syndicate that linked members of the Lebanese diaspora in North and South America and Nigeria with partners in their Mediterranean homeland.[142] In January 2011, a Lebanese national, Ayman Joumaa, was placed on a U.S. Treasury Department Office of Foreign Asset Control (OFAC) blacklist for cocaine trafficking and money laundering for a network operating in West Africa, Lebanon, Colombia, and Panama.[143]

Hezbollah, an international terrorist group with links to the Lebanese diaspora, relies on independent, transnational criminal specialists in West Africa with close links to the drug trade for money laundering, document forgery, and other criminal activities.[144] Historically, Hezbollah had a significant role in the blood diamond trade. In addition, many in the Lebanese diaspora community in West Africa, numbering several hundred thousand, pay a portion of their earnings to support Hezbollah in Lebanon, with the knowledge and acquiescence of host governments in the subregion. The importance of this revenue stream was revealed when a charter flight bound for Beirut from Cotonou, Benin, crashed on takeoff on December 25, 2003. On board was a Hezbollah "foreign relations" official carrying $2 million in contributions raised in the region.[145]

A DEA investigation into the Lebanese Canadian Bank illustrates why Hezbollah's activities in West

Africa are of concern.[146] In February 2011, the U.S. Department of the Treasury, working with the DEA, listed the Lebanese Canadian Bank and its subsidiaries as a financial institution of concern for money laundering. This investigation uncovered a complex scheme that moved illegal drugs from South America to Europe and the Middle East via West Africa and masked the proceeds through sales of used cars and consumer goods.[147] This bank and its subsidiaries were involved in money laundering of hundreds of millions of dollars per month. Its subsidiary in Gambia, Prime Bank, is owned by a Lebanese national believed to be a Hezbollah supporter.[148] Treasury found complex links between the bank and drug traffickers to Hezbollah. (Treasury and the DEA were also able to link individuals in Iran to this criminal money laundering and drug smuggling network.[149])

4. **Iran.** Because of a possible link to terrorism financing, the DEA has targeted on a priority basis Iranian distribution networks involved in sending heroin to West Africa for onward shipment to the United States. In May 2010, an investigation involving the DEA office in Accra, Ghana, resulted in the seizure of 80 kgs of heroin contained in eight industrial metal gears that had arrived via air cargo from Tehran, Iran. In November 2010, a joint investigation by the DEA and the Nigerian Drug Law Enforcement Agency resulted in the seizure of 118 kgs of Southwest Asian (SWA) heroin in a commercial shipping container originating in Iran. In June 2011, the DEA Paris Office, in coordination with the French Customs Service, searched a crate which led to the discovery of two 200-gram packages of heroin contained within each of the 26 cylinders, for a total net weight of 10.4 kgs of

heroin. The shipment from Iran was going to transit Paris on its way to West Africa.[150]

IMPACT ON GOOD GOVERNANCE

UN Secretary General Ban Ki-Moon, speaking before the UN Security Council in February 2012 about peace, security, and stability in West Africa and the Sahel, stated that:

> Transnational organized crime, including drug trafficking, affects peace, security and stability wherever it occurs. It undermines the authority and effectiveness of State institutions, erodes the rule of law and weakens law enforcement structures.[151]

Secretary General Ban is correct to be concerned about West Africa. Some analysts believe that the damage done to governance in West Africa due to the drug trade has already reached the point that some governments in the subregion are "dominated by criminal networks,"[152] and that their sovereignty and even viability as independent rule of law based entities is in jeopardy.[153] As UNODC put it, West African states:

> . . . risk becoming shell-states; sovereign in name, but hollowed out from the inside by criminals in collusion with corrupt officials in the government and the security services. This not only jeopardized their survival, it poses a serious threat to regional security because of the trans-national nature of the crimes.[154]

In short, these violent nonstate actors may represent, over time, an existential threat to the viability of West African states and thus the greatest challenge to human security in the subregion since resource conflicts rocked several countries starting in the early-1990s.

"Narco-Corruption" Fuels Coups D'État, Buys Political Power/Protection.

There is little doubt that the proceeds of drug trafficking are indeed fueling a dramatic increase in narco-corruption in West Africa. UNODC indicated in a 2010 report that the drug trade in West Africa appears to be controlled by national figures so powerful that little opposition is possible, but where disputes over illicit markets "can lead to the toppling of governments."[155] Mauritanian national Ahmedou Ould Abdallah—the UN's former Special Representative of the Secretary General for West Africa, Somalia, and Burundi—stated in a February 2012 interview that "several West African leaders, through family ties or their own contacts, were connected to the drug trade in the region." He felt that politics in West Africa already had "gangrene" because of drug corruption and that:

> One can imagine the problems that Westerners will have working with the countries of West Africa in a few years—if not now—when one sees how much trouble the United States is having now working with Latin America [on the drug issue].[156]

With the presence of large amounts of money, drug traffickers can stage coups d'état, hijack elections, and buy political power. In Guinea-Bissau, at least the last two coups d'état have been directly or indirectly linked to a fight for control of the drug trade. In drug trafficking hubs such as Ghana and Nigeria, members of Parliament, police officials, and government ministers have been implicated in drug smuggling over the past year.[157] The largest seizure of heroin in New York in 2006 was made from a shipment originating from Ghana and belonging to a Ghanaian member of parliament who was not subsequently suspended from his position in government.[158] In January 2011, then Ghanaian President Atta-Mills called in Western diplomats for a private meeting at which he reassured them of Ghana's resolve in the fight against illicit drugs in order to dissipate doubts following revelations that Ghana's national drug bureau had actively collaborated with drug traffickers to torpedo a United Kingdom (UK) anti-drug operation involving cocaine and heroin transiting Ghana en route to the UK.[159] Drug trafficking is a major problem for the Government of Sierra Leone—a recovering failed state at risk of regression because of illicit drugs.[160] In Sierra Leone, the Minister of Transportation resigned after his brother was implicated in the country's largest cocaine seizure,[161] but was rehired despite this scandal.[162] In Mauritania, the son of former President Ould Haidalla was arrested on cocaine-trafficking charges.[163]

Framing the seriousness of the governance challenge, one academic wrote recently that:

> Cocaine trafficking is becoming integral to how West Africa is governed. Political actors are using criminal organization as an aspect of statecraft, and criminal actors are using political privileges as business assets. Traffickers get access to state immunities, passport and diplomatic bags, airspace and maritime approaches, and even state-owned vessels. National political and military institutions are in turn used to tax the trade.[164]

One Ghanaian academic recently said that narcotics were the top challenge now facing West Africa, both for "functional states" such as Ghana, and "nonfunctional" states such as Guinea-Bissau.[165] Worsening the situation is the fact that many ruling elites in West Africa, fearing internal coups and yet facing little threat of external aggression, systematically allowed their militaries to deteriorate in the years after independence.[166] These elites also kept their law enforcement and justice systems underdeveloped and corrupt, with police chiefs in many West African countries being appointed directly by the president and dependent on the head of state's support and patronage for resources, promotion, and the job itself.[167] Drug traffickers are able to offer law enforcement officials in West Africa more than they could earn in a lifetime simply to look the other way.[168] Some ruling elites are even tempted to use anti-drug campaigns as a mechanism to weaken political opposition.[169] Anti-corruption bodies have also been very weak, often serving as yet another mechanism for purging domestic opposition instead of cleaning up deficient institutions.[170]

UNODC's current Representative for West Africa said in June 2011 that a big part of the problem is a weakness in the subregion of the judicial and penal systems, where there remains a "culture of impunity." Up to then, he added, no country in West Africa had ever brought a case in its judicial system for laundering drug money. This representative asserted that the international community had focused its efforts on law enforcement, and had done little to strengthen the judicial systems.[171] Consistent with this, a French national was convicted in Nouakchott, Mauritania, in February 2010, along with a police commissioner, a former International Criminal Police Organization (INTERPOL) representative, and local businessman, of transporting 760 kilos of cocaine in a minibus in August 2007. In August 2011, however, the court of appeals reversed the convictions and freed the accused. In September 2011, the Mauritania Supreme Court reversed the appeals court decision, fired the head of the appeals court, and punished four other judges for their decision to reverse the convictions.[172]

Even when officials are not corrupt, state-paid prosecutors are usually no match for the best defense lawyers that drug money can buy.[173] Not surprisingly, when drug trafficking surges, the legal system becomes overburdened with court cases related to drugs in one way or another—when there are even applicable laws in place to indict individuals, let alone prosecute and incarcerate them.

Drugs—A New Form of Resource Conflict?

In the post-independence period in West Africa, much of political conflict focused on gaining access to the state in order to control rents from various legal, semi-illegal, or outright illegal resource economies— such as diamonds, gold and other precious metals, stones, and timber (Liberia, and Sierra Leone), oil (Nigeria) and fishing. The latter is often conducted illegally and destructively by international fleets from outside West Africa.[174] Since the early-1990s, this conflict in West Africa devolved into protracted violent clashes and civil wars that, as one academic testified:

> centered on natural resources, particularly diamonds, timber, oil, and gold. Profits from these resource wars

fueled the rise of the Revolutionary United Front (RUF) in Sierra Leone, for example, fed the wars sustained by Liberia's Charles Taylor and contributed to the rampant corruption and weak or failed institutions in almost every country of the sub-region. At the same time, these kinds of natural resources, while valuable, pale in comparison to the money now generated by the cocaine trade in West Africa. For example, at its peak, the total annual value of the 'blood diamond' trade smuggled out of Sierra Leone and Liberia was less than $200 million. . . . The potential to fuel conflicts over the cocaine pipeline, the most lucrative commodity so far and one whose profits are several orders of magnitude larger than diamonds, is truly frightening. . . . Just as the 'blood diamond' trade and illicit timber deals allowed groups like the RUF to purchase advanced weapons on the international market, the influx of cocaine cash will allow the criminal and militia groups in the region to acquire ever more sophisticated armaments, training, and communications.[175]

Separatists in Senegal's Casamance Region are already using the drug trade to finance their rebellion, and while they have historically used the sale of cannabis to do so,[176] it is logical to assume that cocaine revenues will eventually contribute to this ongoing instability, if they have not already.

Even if West Africa does not see a return of civil wars or rebellions, diplomats and other international officials worry that some West African countries could develop "along similar lines to Mexico, where drug gangs have a symbiotic relationship with political parties and with the state and drug-related violence results in thousands of deaths every year."[177] The current UNODC Representative for Mexico, Antonio Mazzitelli, who was also previously its representative for West Africa, believes that West Africa could see far greater violence, much like "small gangs in Jamaica," such as those by drug kingpin Christopher "Dudus" Coke, who was extradited to the United States in 2010.[178] One academic hypothesized that where there is political sponsorship of drug trafficking, violence can be relatively low, but that:

> ... where sponsorship is contested, violence results. In January 2011, for example, a major battle was fought between Berabiche Arabs running drugs to Libya, and Touareg [tribesmen] who demanded a fee for passing through their territory.[179]

Latin American drug gangs themselves could also be the source of killings and other violence in West Africa, adding to the region's instability. Many of the Mexican cartel wars are, in essence, resource wars, with the merchandise in dispute being not only the trafficked drugs but the physical trafficking hubs through which the illicit goods must pass. In other words, the criminal pipeline itself can become a resource in dispute, and one of the primary sources of violence.[180] There is also a risk that rivalries between various African networks of corrupt politicians or military officials could lead to violence—something some analysts believe has already occurred in Guinea-Bissau.

Whether similar cartel wars could break out in Africa is uncertain. Some skeptics assert that such violence would not be consistent with the way disputes are handled in West Africa; it may also be the case that governance is so weak that there are multiple channels or pipelines to traffic through the subregion's 16 countries, and therefore little reason to fight over them. One exception, however, could involve fighting for control of choice island landing strips in Guinea-Bissau, which, with the collusion of a weak host government, are particularly valuable pipelines.

Civil society can also be intimidated and muzzled by the drug trade. There have been significant instances of interference with the freedom of the press by some officials in Guinea-Bissau related to media reports on drug trafficking and alleged related corruption in the military. According to the report of the UN Secretary General on the mission to Guinea-Bissau in September 2007:

> The period from July to August 2007 was marked by tensions over concerns by civil society organizations regarding what they saw as pressures relating to freedom of the press and freedom of expression in connection with their reports on drug trafficking.

A November 2007 report from Reporters Without Borders recounts how Guinea-Bissau journalists had received death threats from senior military officials. One brave Ghanaian investigative journalist released an undercover video showing numerous customs agency officials taking bribes at Tema Harbor in February 2012.[181] Human rights can also become a casualty when drug traffickers are calling the shots.[182]

Drug Trade Not a Threat to Political Stability?

One contrarian—and some would say cynical—view is that it is incorrect to assume that "the drug trade epidemic" in West Africa will necessarily challenge political stability and threaten existing governments. One academic has written that, "To the extent that a governing elite captures rents from the drug trade, a symbiosis between foreign (and national) drug traffickers and the ruling elites may develop"[183]—analogous to what has occurred in Jamaica.[184]

In this view, drug traffickers enjoy a sponsored safe haven, and the stability of the existing political status quo is reinforced—making it harder to root out these entrenched interests.[185]

The fundamental problem with this view, however, is that the short-term stability of having nondemocratic ruling elites enter into "symbiotic" relationships with drug traffickers will in the long-term choke off democratic evolution in West Africa. The stability of this alliance lasts only until the next group of wannabe leaders acts to mount a coup or launch an insurgency—thereby perpetuating a new form of resource conflict in West Africa. Guinea-Bissau's instability is evidence of this point in terms of this nation having a briefly stable "alliance" over the drug proceeds that became unsustainable as different segments then started to compete for control of this illicit trade.

Guinea-Bissau—Already a Narco-State.

In West Africa, Guinea-Bissau is generally recognized as a narco-state where state-capture has already occurred.[186] A "narco-state" has been defined as a nation that has been taken over and is controlled and corrupted by drug cartels and where law enforcement is effectively nonexistent.[187] In Guinea-Bissau, drug trafficking networks penetrated the highest levels of power, including the office of former President Joao Bernardo Vieira, who was assassinated in March 2009. As a result of such corruption, the narcotics trade flourished and likely now surpasses the entire formal value of the national economy.[188] Military leaders have since been designated "drug kingpins" by the U.S. Government. Ex-Navy Chief of Staff Jose Americo Bubo Na Tchuto, for example, was listed as a drug kingpin in April 2010 by the U.S. Department of the Treasury,[189]and then reinstated by the Guinea-Bissau government as the head of the Navy a few months later. Armed Forces Chief Antonio Injai reportedly had been competing with Tchuto for a larger share of drug profits,[190] with the former controlling airports, and the latter, maritime shipments.[191] Ibrahima Camara, the head of Guinea-Bissau's air force, is also involved in drug trafficking. One observer believes that the involvement of the Guinea-Bissau armed forces in the drug trade is so entrenched that there exists a generational tension between an old guard that has access to drug revenues, and a younger generation of officers that wants its share.[192]

One researcher has argued that Guinea-Bissau is most consistent with a failed state, *not* a narco-state. This researcher argues that, while certain organs of the state in Guinea-Bissau may have been captured through narco-corruption (the military and criminal justice sector), one cannot say that the capacity of the state has been altered, because of its extremely limited capacity to begin with.[193] This researcher's distinction, while more definitional than substantive, may nevertheless be useful because it implies that international assistance to Guinea-Bissau's police authorities may help create a beachhead within the state against narco-corruption. While weak compared to the military, police authorities, in alliance with civil society, could help lead a fight in the future to recapture Guinea-Bissau from narco-traffickers.

Both the United States and the broader international community, through the UN, are working to assist police and judicial authorities in Guinea-Bissau. Guinea-Bissau's Transnational Crime Unit (TCU) was the result of work that UNODC started in 2008 with the Guinea-Bissau Judicial Police to set up a specialized unit to increase the number of investigations into drug trafficking and organized crime.[194] The TCU was expanded in 2011 to branches of the Judicial Police in two key remote locations of the country: the Island of Bubaque in the Bijagós Archipelago and Catió in the south of Guinea-Bissau. UNODC has also worked to strengthen the justice system and rule of law structures, most notably by training judges and prosecutors specializing in cases related to drug trafficking and organized crime.[195]

Assistant Secretary of State Johnnie Carson, in a May 2012 Senate testimony, listed three key lines of efforts for the United States in Guinea-Bissau needed to fight drug trafficking, beyond working to restore civilian authority and constitutional rule of law. The first was to work alongside international partners in applying targeted sanctions (e.g., travel bans and asset freezes) on the worst or most vulnerable offenders. The second was to continue to pursue security sector reform in Guinea-Bissau — to remove corrupt elements from its military, strengthen law enforcement, and instill respect for civilian government. Third was to pursue a policy of "containment" by helping Guinea-Bissau's neighbors improve the capacity of their customs, border, and port authorities.[196]

With regard to Assistant Secretary Carson's second key line of effort, the U.S. Department of State's Bureau of International Narcotics and Law Enforcement Affairs (INL) funded two new positions in June 2011, dedicated to Guinea-Bissau: a Regional Law Enforcement Advisor and a Justice Sector Advisor. The Regional Law Enforcement Advisor is based in Benin. The Advisor developed a long-term law enforcement training strategy and coordinated U.S. Government assistance to Guinea-Bissau law enforcement agencies.[197] In November 2011, INL and the UN Integrated Peace-Building Office in Guinea-Bissau collaborated on Guinea-Bissau's first "National Forum on Criminal Justice." The forum issued a report that recommended a substantial restructuring of the nation's criminal justice system and changes to the criminal code.[198]

Guinea as the Next Narco-State?

Some observers fear that the next state in West Africa at risk of capture by drug traffickers is Guinea-Conakry, the eastern neighbor of Guinea-Bissau. Since a coup in Guinea in December 2008, there have been reports of Latin American cocaine traders moving in significant numbers to Conakry, where some relatives of the late President Lansana Ousmane Conte have an established interest in the cocaine trade.[199] In 2010, the U.S. Government designated Ousmane Conte, the son of Guinea's late President, as a Tier I Kingpin.[200] Although Alpha Condé became Guinea's first democratically elected President in November 2010, his tenure has been weakened by delays in legislative elections and a lack of progress in security sector reform, which has left a bloated military bureaucracy that is more interested in its own prerogatives than in fighting against the drug trade. As with Guinea-Bissau, the international community urgently needs to work together with the Condé government to turn the tide against state-capture in Guinea by drug traffickers.

IMPACT ON SOCIETY

Historically, the societies of transit countries have never been able to remain immune from the negative impacts of drug trafficking. Inevitably, local consumption of drugs increases, which has cascading negative effects on the social fabric, stability, and security of any transit country.[201] For example, no country in Latin America has suffered as much as Brazil for becoming a key transit country, where payment is often made with drugs; it has become the second largest consumer of cocaine in the world, after the United States.[202] Already, West Africa is proving that it is no exception. There is often a lack of appreciation by leaders in West Africa of how serious this problem is, and of how rapidly it can metastasize. An estimated $800 million was spent on drug use in 2009 alone in West Africa, which has become a huge local consumption market.[203] Drug consumption in West and Central Africa is growing quickly, with up to 2.5 million estimated drug users now in these areas, a UN official reported in February 2012.[204]

There are roughly 1.1 million cocaine consumers in West Africa, according to UNODC, which indicates that 8 percent of the world's 14 million cocaine users are from the subregion.[205] Of the 35 tons of cocaine that transited West Africa en route to Europe in 2010, 13 tons were consumed locally, and somewhat less than one ton seized.[206] Of particular concern is crack cocaine—increasingly popular due to the yield of 30-40 doses of crack cocaine from one gram of pure cocaine. The numbers of crack cocaine users have increased considerably over the past few years.[207]

UNODC estimated in 2009 that there were 793,000 heroin users in Central and West Africa, and 1.7 million for the continent as a whole.[208]

Trafficking has also fueled increasing consumption of methamphetamine in the subregion.[209] ATS are transported mainly from Nigeria to several countries in West Africa, with traffickers using land routes due to the free movement policy of ECOWAS. The use of amphetamines has already been reported in several West African countries, including Burkina Faso, Niger, Senegal, and Sierra Leone—even among school-aged children. UNODC has established an annual prevalence rate of amphetamines at 1.4 percent in Nigeria based on a 2008 household survey. This rate is higher than South Africa, currently thought of as the most established ATS market in Africa, higher than in most European countries, and comparable to use levels in Asia, where ATS use has a long tradition.[210]

Ghana is one example of a West African nation with a growing illicit drug problem. Cannabis is the most abused illicit drug, but the use of hard drugs is on the rise. Cocaine and heroin are the upper-middle-class drugs of choice, while poorer Ghanaians get hooked on crack cocaine.[211] Evidence of an increase in cocaine and heroin usage in Ghana is the sharp increase in requests for drug recovery treatment in 2011. Up to June 2011, there were 887 illicit drug users being treated at four psychiatric hospitals, with 7 percent being treated for cocaine abuse, 4 percent for heroin abuse, and the remainder for marijuana.[212] It is safe to assume that those seeking treatment at psychiatric hospitals are but a small fraction of local users. Nigeria already has a large number of heroin addicts, who number at least in the tens of thousands.[213] One U.S. Government source had interviewed addicts in Liberia and Sierra Leone who use cocaine, heroin, and crack cocaine, and saw crack cocaine addicts in Guinea-Bissau—evidence that these drugs are being consumed in West Africa in even poorer countries than Ghana and Nigeria.[214]

Throughout West Africa, the presence of drugs is engendering a growing user population and straining already weak health systems with no real mechanisms to cope.[215] Due to the lack of hard data on consumption, it is too early to tell how bad the long-term health implications of drug trafficking through West Africa will be. Despite this, experiences of other transit states tell us they will be serious.[216] For one example, governments in the subregion compromised by drug trafficking have less to invest in health or education because those resources have been diverted to address the insecurity resulting from trafficking-related violence.[217]

Besides drug-related violence and the damage to the health of West Africans, drugs and easy money are also having a corrosive effect on societal norms and values. In Ghana, there is a correlation between increasing levels of addiction and rising crime.[218] Drugs devalue traditional values, which had kept African societies cohesive and united. Unemployed and desperate youths are vulnerable to being recruited as foot soldiers for criminal groups.[219] One ECOWAS report, referring to youth perceptions of drug trafficking indicated:

> Many young people believe that they can get rich quick; they avoid school and end up as unskilled. . . . The associated violence increasingly threatens people's daily lives.[220]

Some West African drug traffickers even justify their criminal activities as a way for the black market to redistribute wealth.[221] One observer noted that major drug traffickers act as heads of patronage networks because of the prestige and influence that this buys, and because of an African expectation that wealth should be shared with each individual's network of family and friends.[222] Rich cocaine pushers who hold extravagant parties to celebrate the acquisition of a chieftancy title are a recognizable social type in West Africa, one sociologist has asserted.[223] To flaunt their status, they build opulent, "narcotecture" homes.[224] In Nigeria, one academic has written, "some individuals have asserted that, since the drug trade involves willing sellers and willing buyers at every stage of the chain, it is essentially a legitimate form of commerce."[225] They use this to justify illegal economies, including the drug trade, and share their profits with local social groups to accumulate substantial political capital and acquire legitimacy.[226] Unfortunately, societal norms in Ghana look favorably upon successful drug traffickers, as their increased wealth is seen as "honorable," one Ghanaian academic has asserted.[227] In local languages, this academic has noted the increased use of proverbs that "glorify this wealth" and make parallels to the honor of "going to war." Some drug dealers are buying royal titles, like "development chief," to gain social status, and wearing Ghanaian traditional kente cloth with gold jewelry. There is a "billionaire boys" club in Accra, some of whose members drive Maseratis. This academic believed that the best way to fight drug trafficking and its social acceptance is by the "naming and shaming" of drug traffickers. [228]

IMPACT ON THE ECONOMY

A few observers do not see the net economic impact of the drug trade on West Africa as all bad. Some say that illicit drug trafficking in West Africa — by far

the most lucrative transnational criminal activity[229] —
has become institutionalized and so entrenched that
it is essentially a part of each country's economy,
making a huge, though unofficial, contribution to
national income.[230]

Indeed, trafficking in heroin, cocaine, and amphetamines has expanded dramatically across Africa as a
whole, growing into a roughly $6-7 billion annual il-
licit industry, according to conservative estimates.[231]
Estimates vary widely on the amount of drug money
flowing specifically into the subregion of West Africa.
In 2007, UNODC conservatively estimated that 40-50
tons of cocaine, with an estimated value of $1.8 bil-
lion, passed through West Africa.[232] By contrast, it is
estimated that the amount of cocaine transiting West
Africa was at least five times the UNODC figure.[233]
At a May 2012 hearing, U.S. Senator Charles Grassley
estimated that cocaine flowing through West Africa
ranged between 60 and 250 metric tons, with annual profits estimated between $3 billion and $14 billion. These profits, the Senator noted, easily eclipsed
the value of the legitimate economies of most West
African countries.[234]

The only non-oil legal export from the region of
greater value than cocaine is cocoa, primarily from
Cote d'Ivoire. The value of cocaine transiting West
Africa surpasses even gold exports from Ghana and
bauxite exports from Guinea.[235] Besides oil-rich Nigeria, criminal proceeds from drug trafficking in West
Africa probably average about 10 percent of typical
government revenues—which indicates how under-
resourced most West African governments are compared to TOC groups. The worst case is Guinea-Bissau,
whose status as the region's leading cocaine hub means
that the value of its trafficking economy exceeds its tiny
formal economy.[236]

Drug trafficking may be the most important variable that explains empirical data suggesting that:

> cash remittances from Europe have increased dramatically in recent years in a number of West African countries. In Cote d'Ivoire, Ghana, Nigeria, and Senegal, as examples, there has been a doubling or tripling of remittances.[237]

While all these countries have large expatriate populations, this sudden growth is difficult to explain without reference to the illicit drug trade. The currency of one small West African nation, Gambia, experienced a rapid appreciation of its value starting at the end of July 2007. The *dalasi* appreciated 25.9 percent in value against the dollar in one single day on September 27, 2007[238] — likely due to money laundering related to a new hub for the cocaine trade that was reportedly set up in Gambia after (temporary) disruptions in Guinea-Bissau and Guinea.[239] In June 2010, concrete evidence of the link to Guinea-Bissau and money flooding the economy came in the form of the arrest in Gambia of five Venezuelans — one of whom confessed to having moved from Guinea-Bissau — and in the seizure of 2,196 kilos of cocaine with a street value of $1 billion — about half of Gambia's annual gross national product in 2010. Gambian authorities, with the help of UK anti-drug officials, also arrested a Dutch national of Lebanese origin.[240]

Because the scale of the illicit drug trade in West Africa is unknown, its exact contribution to each country's gross domestic product (GDP) is unknown. Most analysts, however, conclude that being a drug transit state is, on net, very detrimental to a country's development.[241] Economically, the influx of drug and other dirty monies into the local market can seem like a balm on poverty in the short term. There may be a building boom, with construction providing needed jobs and better quality accommodation. Over time, however, much of this money begins to leave the country. Eventually, the tourism and business sectors start to suffer too.[242] Investors are less inclined to do business in drug transit countries because unstable environments are risky and operating in higher-crime areas entails higher business costs.[243] Drug money investments also risk exacerbating inflation and may contribute to high real estate prices that disadvantage those engaged in licit economic activities. TOC also hinders development in other ways by undermining the rule of law, governance, the environment, and health.[244]

ONGOING PROGRAMS—
THE INTERNATIONAL COMMUNITY
AND THE UNITED STATES

Given West Africa's underdevelopment and the global nature of drug trafficking, it is clear that the governments of the subregion cannot respond to this problem—and illicit trafficking in general—without the help and cooperation of regional organizations and the international community. West African nations, for the most part, welcome the aid and cooperation of the international community. Benin President Boni Yayi, for example, wrote in July 2011 to UN Secretary General Ban Ki-Moon to request UNODC's assistance in helping his country formulate a national integrated program to fight drug trafficking and organized crime.[245] Togo President Faure Gnassingbe also reportedly sees the drug trade as a threat to his authority.[246]

Some observers have argued that basic government, law enforcement, and military institutions must be in place before substantial investment in operational hardware will benefit West African nations.[247] One case in point is that of the national agencies in West Africa charged with counternarcotics missions. Many do not know how to gather and analyze counterdrug intelligence, nor how to conduct investigations. Most of the big seizures in West Africa have occurred by chance or through a foreign tip-off. Many governments also do not have the legal systems, judicial structures, plans, funding, resources, and political will to combat drugs. Many countries lack the legal concepts of conspiracy and plea bargaining. Both are powerful legal tools in combating organized crime.[248] Until recently, authorities have not systematically used asset seizures from traffickers and money launderers as enforcement tools.[249]

Ongoing programs by the UN, EU, and the United States to aid West Africa's anti-narcotics efforts include the following.

UN/EU Assistance.

International aid to West Africa's war on drugs is only in an initial stage. In 2008, ECOWAS, supported by UNODC and the UN Office for West Africa (UN-OWA), in partnership with the EU, held a Ministerial Conference in Cape Verde to analyze the security threat posed by drug trafficking in the region. The action plan that resulted from this conference was subsequently endorsed by ECOWAS Heads of State and contained five thematic areas:

1. Mobilization of ECOWAS political leadership;
2. Effective law enforcement and national/ regional cooperation;

3. Appropriate and adequate legal frameworks;

4. Emerging threats of drug abuse and associated health and security problems; and,

5. Reliable data to assess the magnitude of the drug trafficking and abuse problems.[250]

The West Africa Coast Initiative (WACI), officially launched in December 2009, was the UN's response to the priorities in the ECOWAS Regional Action Plan and is part of the UN's Regional Program for West Africa for 2010-14. WACI and the Regional Program are designed to support the efforts of West African States, regional organizations, and the civil society to respond to evolving security threats and to promote the rule of law and good governance. Within the UN family of agencies, WACI is a joint program of UNODC, UN-OWA, the Department of Political Affairs (DPA), and the Department of Peacekeeping Operations (DPKO), joined by INTERPOL, which is not part of the UN.

WACI's overall strategy, which is initially being implemented in select West African countries, is to strengthen the capacity of law enforcement officials at both the national and subregional levels to combat drug trafficking and organized crime. WACI targets institutional capacity, building in law enforcement, forensics, border management, money laundering, criminal justice institutions, peace-building initiatives, and security sector reform. It provides equipment, technical assistance, and specialized training. WACI's initial phase of assistance involved an assessment of the capacities and needs of four pilot countries where there was already a major UN presence: Côte d'Ivoire, Guinea-Bissau, Liberia, and Sierra Leone. This initial phase was concluded in February 2010 by a Ministerial Conference in Sierra Leone, where Ministers of the

Interior of the four pilot countries adopted the Freetown Commitment and pledged to support WACI implementation. A cornerstone of WACI is the establishment of elite TCUs in each country. These act as national focal points for international cooperation, and bring together police, customs, and immigration officers, prosecutors, and INTERPOL National Central Bureaus, and also have access to INTERPOL's I-24/7 communications network and global police databases.[251]

Several other UN programs, such as the 2010 Airport Communication Project (AIRCOP) sponsored by the EU and Canada, have been developed to attack drug trafficking. One AIRCOP operation, Cocair 3, resulted in nearly 50 arrests, the seizure of more than 500 kgs of drugs, and the recovery of 2.5 million euros in cash at 25 airports across Western and Central Africa and Brazil.[252] During its presidency of the G8, France sponsored a meeting in March 2011 of G8 members, with representatives from West Africa, Morocco, Algeria, South Africa, and several Latin American and European nations to discuss the growing problem of drug trafficking through Africa and a possible financing mechanism through the World Bank.[253]

U.S. Assistance.

U.S. counternarcotics assistance to West Africa is also still in an early stage, but complements ongoing efforts by the UN, the EU, and other international actors. American counternarcotics assistance for West Africa totaled about $50 million for 2010 and 2011, up from just $7.5 million in 2009.[254] The U.S. Government is just starting its West Africa Cooperative Security Initiative (WACSI) program, which will partner with the international donor community to engage ECOWAS and support its Regional Action Plan.[255] In this context, the U.S. Department of State sponsored a February 2012 meeting on the margins of the G8 Roma-Lyon Group in Washington to discuss engagement with ECOWAS, share program plans for the year, and discuss review mechanisms for sustained donor coordination. Besides UNODC and the EU, other participant countries were Canada, Colombia, France, Germany, Italy, Japan, Mexico, Russia, Spain, and the UK.

WACSI is a 5-year, whole of government program, developed in accordance with U.S. President Obama's *Strategy to Combat Transnational Organized Crime*, to address drug trafficking and organized crime in West Africa.[256] WACSI will help ECOWAS member-states to harmonize their anti-drug and crime laws. In some countries, such as Ghana and Nigeria, U.S. assistance will focus on building capacity to detect, disrupt, and dismantle drug trafficking networks. A U.S. judicial adviser is being sent to Ghana, for example, to provide training and advice on the prosecution of complex drug cases. In other countries, especially post-conflict countries like Liberia and Sierra Leone, WACSI aims to enhance basic law enforcement.[257] Starting later in 2012, an experienced U.S. prosecutor will serve as a legal advisor in Sierra Leone to assist that country in its efforts to combat public corruption more effectively, including by supporting investigations and prosecutions.[258]

Some observers have described WACSI as an initiative that will try to replicate the steps taken in battling trafficking groups operating in Central America and Mexico. U.S. Assistant Secretary of State for International Narcotics and Law Enforcement William Brownfield said the vision for both Central America and West Africa was to improve the ability of nations to deal with drug trafficking, by building up their own institutions and getting them to cooperate with one another, sharing intelligence, and running regional law enforcement training centers.[259]

U.S. Government agencies have taken several other steps to address illicit drug trafficking in West Africa, some of which can be considered part of WACSI:

- DEA: In West Africa, the DEA currently has offices in Nigeria and Ghana, and plans to open a future office in Senegal.[260] During FY 2011, the DEA organized eight seminars in Africa for 244 African law enforcement personnel, including working through the Department of State's International Law Enforcement Academy (ILEA) in Botswana.[261] The DEA, partnering with Ghanaian authorities, aided the establishment in August 2010 of the Ghana Vetted Unit—the first vetted SIU in Africa. Due to its success, the Ghana Vetted Unit was accepted into the DEA's global SIU program in August 2011. In 2012, the DEA worked with Nigerian authorities to establish a vetted unit in Lagos.[262] The DEA has requested funding from Congress for additional offices and SIUs in other African countries, including in West Africa.[263]
- State Department: In countries where there is not yet a strong understanding of the domestic implications of being a transit state, the State Department hopes to use public diplomacy to build awareness[264] among the population, and particularly youth, regarding addiction and the long-term health effects of drug use.[265]
- DoD: The DoD Counternarcotics Strategy, which guides counternarcotics operations

and assistance at all Combatant Commands, including AFRICOM, calls for building host-nation capacity to conduct counternarcotics operations through "enhancement of interdiction forces."[266] Training topics include airport interdiction, clandestine methamphetamine lab training, money laundering, and investigatory skills.[267]

- AFRICOM: AFRICOM's Counter Narcotics and Law Enforcement Division provides about $20 million in annual assistance to African partner nations to help build their capacity to combat transnational narcotics trafficking.[268] Country project officers and intelligence analysts from AFRICOM are actively collaborating with their counterparts at Joint Interagency Task Force South (JIATF-S), based at the U.S. Southern Command in Miami, Florida, the U.S. Office of Naval Intelligence, the Defense Intelligence Agency, the EU's Maritime Analysis Operations Center (MAOC) based in Lisbon, Portugal, and others to monitor the drug flow, support the broader efforts, build capacity, and help guide which projects will have the greatest impact against drug trafficking organizations. AFRICOM also provides assistance to African military and law enforcement units with counternarcotics missions, and has the following projects already underway in West Africa:
  — Students from multiple West African nations attend courses taught by U.S. Coast Guard Trainers;[269]
  — Construction of, and support for, the Cape Verde Counternarcotics and Maritime Security Interagency Operations Center (COSMAR), an interagency fusion center in

49

Praia that develops a regional intelligence picture and communicates with JIATF-S in Miami and MAOC in Lisbon.[270] The facility helped interdict about 1.5 metric tons of cocaine valued at over $100 million in October 2011;[271]

— Construction of a pier and refueling facility to extend the range of the Senegalese Navy to carry out interdiction patrols;

— Construction of a ship maintenance and docking facility in Ghana to assist with maritime drug interdiction. Also, the building for the Navy of a maritime territorial waters monitoring center.[272]

• USAID: The Agency for International Development (USAID) implements democracy and governance programs in West Africa that address some of the key governance considerations related to TOC, including justice sector strengthening and anticorruption efforts. USAID has also commissioned analytic research to better understand the relationship between development and drug trafficking.

IMPACT OF WEST AFRICAN DRUG TRAFFICKING ON U.S. NATIONAL INTERESTS

Beyond counterterrorism, U.S. national security goals for Africa outlined in National Security Presidential Directive (NSPD) 50 include building capacity, consolidating democratic transition, and bolstering fragile states.[273] The growing problem of transnational drug trafficking in West Africa directly jeopardizes related U.S. foreign and economic policy goals in Africa, such as the promotion of legitimate economic growth, state institution-building, and diverse other foreign aid program goals.[274] West Africa is also of increased importance to U.S. national security interest as a growing market and source of energy imports.[275]

One priority for the United States and the international community should be to disrupt the most dangerous networks, i.e., those with the greatest links or potential links to international terrorist groups.[276] Consistent with the priority of disrupting the most dangerous networks, Senator Dianne Feinstein, during a Senate hearing that she chaired in May 2012, gave the following as her two top reasons why fighting the narcotics trade in West Africa is in the U.S. national security interest:

> First, the same Latin American drug trafficking organizations that smuggle cocaine and other illegal drugs into the United States are operating in West Africa, particularly the Colombian FARC. As we support the Colombian government in combating the FARC, it is certainly not in our interest to see them enriched through illicit activities in West Africa. The same is true of Mexican drug trafficking organizations. In 2011, a Lebanese drug kingpin linked to Hezbollah was indicted in U.S. federal court for coordinating the sale of cocaine to Los Zetas by using West Africa to launder huge amounts of drug money, likely up to $200 million a month.

> Second, drug trafficking in West Africa provides financing to dangerous terrorist organizations, such as Al Qaida in the Lands of the Islamic Maghreb, or AQIM. As just one example, in 2010, Mauritanian authorities reported that members of AQIM were providing security for a convoy of cocaine and marijuana.

We must do everything we can to ensure that AQIM and other extremist groups are not further strengthened by the drug trade.[277]

CONCLUSION: POLICY RECOMMENDATIONS

This Paper started with a quote from former UN Secretary General Koffi Annan, who urged the international community "to take action now before the grip of the criminal networks linked to the trafficking of illicit drugs tightened into a stranglehold on West African political and economic development." It then sketched out the context and history of drug trafficking in the region; analyzed the ways DTOs are structured and evolving patterns in trafficking; exposed the negative impact of drugs on West Africa's good governance, society, and economy; reviewed international and U.S. counternarcotics efforts; and explained impacts on U.S. national interests.

In this concluding section, the author will outline, with minimal commentary, several recommendations for U.S. policymakers. None of the recommendations will be easy to implement. All will require budgetary and manpower resources in an era when both will be increasingly scarce. Until recently, the United States, preoccupied by September 11, 2001, and wars in Afghanistan and Iraq, dedicated too few resources to monitoring, much less combating, TOCs in West Africa. Nevertheless, West Africa merits U.S. support, both for the well-being of its citizens, and for those in the United States who will suffer indirectly if the United States does not act now to stop transnational criminal networks operating in the subregion and elsewhere.

Recommendations.

1. Expand the U.S. Government's Physical Presence in the Subregion. The expanded presence of U.S. Government officials in West Africa could allow more efficient and effective collaboration with host-government officials and civil society there by taking the following actions:

   a. Reopen the U.S. Embassy in Guinea-Bissau, and exercise expeditionary diplomacy to facilitate in-country, whole of government cooperation with local authorities and civil society against drug trafficking. Current legislative proscriptions notwithstanding, seek funding/authorization to re-establish a physical presence by official Americans, including by the DEA, if possible, in order to engage the host government and civil society, support police and judicial authorities, and help decriminalize/professionalize the Guinea-Bissau armed forces. At present, the U.S. Embassy is considered "closed," and there is only a limited physical presence of a small number of non-American employees (mainly or entirely Guinea-Bissau nationals, who are considered to be "locally employed staff"). While the U.S. Government, in part due to U.S. law, has taken a sanctions-based approach to Guinea-Bissau so far, it would do well to reconsider parts of its approach. By placing U.S. personnel in Bissau, such as political officers, public diplomacy officers, USAID development officers, Department of Justice legal advisers, or even DEA staffers, the U.S. Government would have a much better chance of implementing useful programs that could influence Guinea-Bissau's government and civil society. If there are legal impediments to such an action, a change in the law should be considered. While the physical presence of U.S. personnel in Bissau would present risks to their physical safety, these risks are manageable and likely far less than those in other beachheads of U.S. "expeditionary diplomacy," such as in Afghanistan, Iraq, and Pakistan.

b. Open a new DEA Office in Dakar (Congress has already been notified, and the office is expected to open in 2013) and consider new offices, e.g., in Bissau or Conakry, Guinea (location to be determined in part by an assessment of the political will in each country to take action to fight against drug trafficking) or increased staffing for regional offices in Accra and Dakar.

2. Seek Adequate, Multiyear Funding for Anti-Narcotics Efforts in West Africa. Success in the anti-drug effort will not be achieved overnight, but rather will take years of sustained commitment by host governments and the international community. The Senate Caucus on International Narcotics Control held hearings in May 2012 on drug trafficking in West Africa and could be the best advocate in Congress for expanded, multiyear funding to fight the drug trade in West Africa. Congress could concurrently seek expanded legislative authority to allow more flexibility in planning multiyear, anti-drug programs. Funding could specifically be increased for the following:

a. WACSI: WACSI is a U.S. Government inter-agency response to the ECOWAS Regional Action Plan, but needs greater certainty of continued future funding. (See Table 1 for FY 11-13 INL funding.)

Country/Region	FY 2011 Actual	FY 2012 Estimate	FY 2013 Request
Africa Regional (TSCTP)*	2,500	3,500	2,500
Africa Regional (West)	2,433	16,800	13,000
Ghana	500	-	-
Guinea	500	-	-
Liberia	16,000	17,000	15,662
Nigeria	1,250	-	-
Subtotal, Africa	61,368	85,900	74,947

*Trans-Sahara Counterterrorism Partnership.
Source: Money Laundering and Financial Crimes–Country Database, May 2012, U.S. Department of State, Bureau of International Narcotics and Law Enforcement Bureau, p. 34.

Table 1. Department of State (International) Budget ($000) FY 2011–2013 INCLE: Overseas Contingency Operations Budget Allocations ($000).

b. USAID Democracy, Governance, Peace, and Security Program: More resources including both funding and dedicated personnel are needed to expand rule of law, anticorruption focused on grand corruption, security sector reform, and counternarcotics efforts to counteract the destabilizing effect of increased narcotics trafficking in West Africa. Such efforts should target justice and police sectors and strengthen related civil-society capacity.

These efforts could be coordinated through USAID's West African Regional Mission if the peace and security staff is expanded beyond the current personal service contractor focused on TSCTP.

c. U.S. Coast Guard (USCG): to allow: 1) expanded training of West African navies and coast guards, while increasing the number and length of port stops for vessels participating in APS; and, 2) possible periodic patrol/interdiction operations in conjunction with European and African counterparts.

d. DoD: to continue its funding for the Liberian Coast Guard under Operation ONWARD LIBERTY, a program managed by the USCG.

e. DEA: to fund the expansion of SIUs in Nigeria in the short term; other SIUs such as in Senegal, Benin, Togo and Cote d'Ivoire in the medium term; and Guinea and Guinea-Bissau in the longer term.

f. AFRICOM: to expand counternarcotics/illicit trafficking training and equipping efforts under its West Africa Regional Engagement Plan.

3. Seek Closer Partnerships with Domestic, International Agencies on West Africa. Countries in West Africa are among the poorest and least developed in the world and have neither the resources nor the capacity to fight powerful drug traffickers alone. By working regionally, e.g., through ECOWAS, and with international partners, they can eliminate duplication of effort and leverage their collaborative actions. Stronger legal cooperation among West African nations, for example, would enable more effective extra-

dition, mutual legal assistance, and confiscation of the proceeds of crime. Stronger legal cooperation will be meaningless, however, without the political will and capacity to implement legal actions:

> The region's leaders must recognize the stakes and their failure to act is a sign of helplessness or complicity. The international community should reward honest regional leaders with additional counter-narcotics and development assistance, and withdraw from those organizations which are corrupt.[278]

Working contacts must also be strengthened between countries of origin and destination, in South America, Europe, and Asia. For its part, the U.S. Government internally should adopt a strong interagency task force or program to address drug trafficking and externally should seek international partners in Europe, Asia, and Latin America who could work with it and ECOWAS member-states and Mauritania on joint counternarcotics efforts. Specifically, the U.S. Government could:

    a. Formalize short- and long-term joint planning, intelligence, and operational efforts between U.S. Coast Guard, the Joint Interagency Task Force South (JIATF-S) in Miami; AFRICOM headquarters in Stuttgart, Germany, including its Interagency representatives and Counternarcotics Office; and U.S. Naval Forces Africa (NAVAF), based in Naples, Italy.

    b. Expand cooperation with European partners. This would include:

       — Increasing real-time information and intelligence-sharing with the EU's Maritime

Analysis Operations Center (MAOC) in Lisbon;
— Continuing the G8 Roma-Lyon Group dialogue, including exploring whether the World Bank and the African Development Bank could fund programs targeting judicial reform;
— Work with the Fontanot Group, a French-led informal group of EU members that meet on a semi-annual basis to discuss counternarcotics projects in West Africa. The group has developed a database to share information on ongoing projects to maximize international cooperation and minimize duplication of effort. AFRICOM and State Department officials attended the last Fontanot meeting and deepened their coordination;
— Work with Brussels (and Ottawa) to see if other cooperative projects are possible, e.g., building on the success of the EU/Canada Airport Communication Project (AIRCOP).

c. Seek other international partners, such as:
— Japan and Korea to jointly address the increasing problem of methamphetamine production in West Africa for sale in Asia and the United States;
— China to support the maritime capacity of West African navies to carry out coast guard function, including loans and grants of patrol boats;
— Brazil, operationally via JIATF-S, the U.S. Coast Guard, AFRICOM, and NAVAF,

and strategically, through consultations with the U.S. Government led by the State Department's Western Hemisphere, Africa, and INL bureaus. Brazil is already cooperating with African countries, particular with Cape Verde. The United States should seek to collaborate with Brazil and with African lusophone countries, which could pay off in joint work in Guinea-Bissau, for example.

d. Deepen Cooperation with UN Agencies and INTERPOL:

— Continue the excellent collaboration with UNODC and INTERPOL—avoiding duplication of effort, and encouraging expansion of effort in West Africa;

— Expand cooperation with the UN's International Maritime Organization (IMO), including its efforts to work with the Maritime Organization of West and Central Africa (MOWCA) and ECOWAS Transport Ministries. Attempt to align IMO/MOWCA efforts to promote coast guard law enforcement functions and engagements with African military and judiciary/police authorities, which have tended to reject IMO/MOWCA.

4. Aid West Africa to Expand Maritime Domain Awareness and Cooperation. Because of limited resources and a strong, historical priority given to land-based forces, there is only limited maritime domain awareness among littoral states in West Africa. Most countries suffer from severe "sea blindness" about

ongoing illicit activities in their respective territorial waters and Exclusive Economic Zones (EEZs). To help correct this situation, the U.S. Government, and AFRICOM in particular, should:

    a. Support ongoing ECOWAS efforts to develop:

— A maritime cooperation and operational agreement for the Gulf of Guinea with the Economic Community of Central African States (ECCAS);

— A regional maritime strategy and operational capacity in three zones, (E, F, and G) through ongoing technical assistance.

    b. Continue to invest in NAVAF's annual African Partnership Station (APS) program and the *Obangame* and *Sahara Express* exercises, which are carried out with African and European partners. Other contributing programs could include the Africa Maritime Law Enforcement Partnership (AMLEP) program, which is helping to build the maritime law enforcement capacity of West African Navies and Coast Guards.

    c. Replicate in Lagos, Accra, Dakar, and other West African capitals, as appropriate, the Cape Verde model of the Counternarcotics and Maritime Security Interagency Operations Center (COSMAR) in order to link these countries to JIATF-S in Miami and MAOC in Lisbon.

    5. Promote International and Regional Agreements, and Changes in Domestic Law. While the U.S. Government has a Presidential Determination allowing it to work directly with ECOWAS, and AFRICOM has already concluded a Memorandum of Under-

standing (MOU) with ECOWAS that encourages further cooperation, it would be beneficial to both the U.S. Government and ECOWAS if they were able to conclude a regional counterdrug agreement that also facilitated bilateral cooperation with the Community's individual member-states. Specifically, the United States could seek the following:

a. Worldwide, there are 44 maritime counterdrug bilateral agreements or operational procedures in place with the United States. The United States and Europe could explore whether ECOWAS (and ECCAS) would be willing, in the medium term, to sign an accord similar to the Caribbean Regional Maritime Agreement, thereby facilitating U.S. and European interdiction in the territorial waters of West (and Central) Africa, in coordination with African partners; and,

b. Generally speaking, the international community could help West African nations to strengthen: 1) their legal frameworks and enforcement mechanisms against organized crime, money laundering, and corruption; and, 2) their law enforcement agencies' operational capabilities, including air, maritime, and land border controls.[279] More specifically, the international community could help countries in West Africa by providing advice and when possible budgetary support to:

- Better train and pay judges, and construct modern prisons;[280]
- Strengthen their anti-corruption commissions and offices of inspectors general with expanded authority, resources, and legal changes allowing greater autonomy;
- Reform election laws to become more transparent and prevent drug profits from buying elections;[281]

— Modify domestic laws to incorporate key provisions of international anti-drug conventions;[282]
— Help African leaders become more conscious of the severity of the situation; and,
— Foster stronger public awareness of the dangers of drug trafficking and consumption.

One ongoing effort is the Dakar Initiative Against Drugs, involving six countries in West Africa—Senegal, Gambia, Guinea, Cape Verde, Mali, and Guinea-Bissau—which in 2010 launched an effort to harmonize national drug control legislation consistent with international law.[283] Ministers of these six countries, supported by regional and international partners including ECOWAS, France, Spain, and the United States, met in September 2012 in Dakar to consider a draft harmonization law.[284] These countries and partners should adopt this draft law and share their lessons learned with other ECOWAS member-states.

Table 2 analyzes further legal and administrative actions West African governments need to take to strengthen their abilities to fight money laundering and financial crimes. The State Department, working with the U.S. Justice and Treasury Departments, USAID, and U.S. Embassies in the subregion, could assist West Africa to bring its domestic laws closer in conformity with international standards.

Actions by Governments	Criminalized Drug Money Laundering	Criminalized Money Laundering Beyond Drugs	Know Your Customer Provisions	Report Large Transactions	Report Suspicious Transactions	Maintain Records over Time	Disclosure Protection – « Safe Harbor »	Criminalized « Tipping Off »	Cross-Border Transportation of Currency	Financial Intelligence Unit	Intl Law Enforcement Cooperation	System for Identifying/Forfeiting Assets	Arrangements for Asset Sharing	Criminalized Financing of Terrorism	Report Suspected Terrorism Financing	Ability to Freeze Terrorist Assets w/o Delay	States Party to 1988 UN Drug Convention	States Party to Intl. Terror Finance Conv.	States Party to UNTOC	States Party to UNCAC	US or Intl Org Sanctions/Penalties
Benin	Y	Y	N	N	Y	Y	Y	Y	Y	Y	Y	Y	N	N	Y	Y	Y	Y	Y	Y	N
Burkina Faso	Y	Y	Y	Y	Y	Y	Y	Y	N	Y	Y	N	N	Y	Y	Y	Y	Y	Y	Y	N
Cape Verde	Y	Y	Y	Y	Y	Y	Y	N	Y	Y	Y	N	N	N	N	Y	Y	Y	Y	Y	N
Cote d'Ivoire	Y	Y	Y	Y	Y	Y	N	Y	Y	Y	Y	Y	Y	Y	Y	Y	Y	Y	N	N	N
Gambia	Y	Y	Y	Y	Y	Y	Y	Y	Y	Y	Y	Y	N	Y	Y	Y	Y	N	Y	N	N
Ghana	Y	Y	Y	N	Y	Y	Y	Y	Y	Y	Y	Y	N	Y	Y	Y	N	Y	N	Y	N
Guinea	Y	N	N	N	N	N	N	N	Y	N	N	N	N	N	N	N	Y	Y	Y	N	N
Guinea-Bissau	Y	Y	Y	Y	Y	Y	Y	N	N	N	N	Y	Y	Y	N	Y	Y	Y	N	N	Y
Liberia	Y	Y	Y	Y	Y	Y	Y	Y	Y	N	N	N	N	N	N	Y	Y	Y	Y	Y	N
Mali	Y	Y	Y	N	Y	Y	Y	N	N	Y	Y	Y	Y	Y	Y	N	Y	Y	Y	Y	N
Mauritania	Y	Y	Y	Y	Y	Y	Y	Y	Y	Y	Y	Y	Y	Y	Y	Y	Y	Y	Y	Y	Y
Niger	Y	Y	Y	N	Y	Y	Y	Y	Y	Y	Y	N	Y	N	Y	Y	N	Y	Y	Y	N
Nigeria	Y	Y	Y	Y	Y	Y	N	Y	Y	Y	Y	Y	N	Y	Y	N	Y	Y	Y	Y	N
Senegal	Y	Y	Y	N	Y	Y	Y	Y	Y	Y	Y	Y	Y	Y	Y	Y	Y	Y	Y	Y	N
Sierra Leone	Y	Y	Y	Y	Y	Y	Y	Y	Y	Y	Y	N	Y	N	Y	N	Y	Y	N	Y	N
Togo	Y	Y	Y	Y	Y	Y	Y	Y	Y	Y	Y	Y	N	Y	Y	Y	Y	Y	Y	Y	N

"Y" is meant to indicate that appropriate legislation has been enacted to address the captioned items. It does not indicate full compliance with international standards.

Source: Money Laundering and Financial Crimes–Country Database, May 2012, U.S. Department of State, Bureau of International Narcotics and Law Enforcement (INL).

Note: This table includes all 15 members of the Economic Community of West African States (ECOWAS) and Mauritania, which left ECOWAS in 1999.

Table 2. Money Laundering And Financial Crimes In West Africa-2012.

ENDNOTES

1. "Cocaine Trafficking in West Africa: The threat to stability and development (with special reference to Guinea-Bissau)," Vienna, Austria: United Nations Office on Drugs and Crime (UNODC), December 2007. For the purposes of this paper, West Africa is defined as Mauritania and the 15 member-states of the ECOWAS, which are: Benin, Burkina Faso, Cape Verde, Cote d'Ivoire, Gambia, Ghana, Guinea, Guinea-Bissau, Liberia, Mali, Niger, Nigeria, Senegal, Sierra Leone, and Togo.

2. Liana Sun Wyler and Nicolas Cook, "Illegal Drug Trade in Africa: Trends and U.S. Policy," Washington, DC: Congressional Research Service, September 30, 2009, Summary.

3. Thomas Harrigan, Statement for the Record, "Countering Narcotics Threats in West Africa," Washington, DC: Senate Caucus on International Narcotics Control, May 16, 2012, p. 6.

4. *Ibid.*

5. Senator Charles Grassley, Opening Statement, "Drug Trafficking in West Africa," Washington, DC: Senate Caucus on International Narcotics Control, May 16, 2012, p. 1.

6. Davin O'Regan, "Cocaine and Instability in Africa: Lessons from Latin America and the Caribbean," Africa Security Brief, Washington, DC: Africa Center for Security Studies, July 2010, pp. 2, 5.

7. Dr. Vanda Felbab-Brown, "The West African Drug Trade in Context of the Region's Illicit Economies and Poor Governance," Presentation to Conference on Drug Trafficking in West Africa, Arlington, VA, October 14, 2010.

8. Senator Dianne Feinstein, Statement, "Drug Trafficking in West Africa," Washington, DC: Senate Caucus on International Narcotics Control, May 16, 2012, p. 1.

9. Christophe Champin, "Le trafic de cocaïne, d'héroïne et metamphétamine s'entend en Afrique" ("Cocaine, Heroin, and Methamphetamine Trafficking Spreads in Africa"), Christophe

Champin, Radio France International (RFI), Blog Afrique Drogue, March 13, 2012.

10. Christophe Champin, "le Nigeria reste un point névralgique pour le trafic de drogue" (Nigeria Remains a Neuralgic Point for Drug Trafficking), RFI, Blog Afrique Drogue, January 19, 2011.

11. Christophe Champin, "Le continent africain toujours prise par les trafiquants de cocaïne, selon "Organe international de contrôle des stupéfiants" ("The African Continent Remains Overtaken by Cocaine Traffickers According to International Drug Control Body"), RFI, Blog Afrique Drogue, March 3, 2011.

12. "Guyana Officials Seize Drugs Destined for Nigeria," Associated Press, November 29, 2012.

13. "Cocaine Trafficking in West Africa," p. 3.

14. Stephen Ellis, "West Africa's International Drug Trade," *African Affairs*, Vol. 108, No. 431, 2009, p. 172.

15. "West Africa - 2012 ATS Situation Report," UNODC, June 2012, p. 12.

16. UNODC, 2007, p. 17.

17. *Ibid.*, p. 11.

18. Wyler and Cook, summary.

19. Ellis, p. 194.

20. Michael Braun, "Confronting Drug Trafficking in West Africa," Washington, DC: Committee on Foreign Relations Subcommittee on African Affairs, June 23, 2009, p. 3.

21. Johnnie Carson, Testimony, "Countering Narcotics Threats in West Africa," Washington, DC: Senate Caucus on International Narcotics Control, May 16, 2012.

22. Antonio Maria Costa, "Cocaine Finds Africa," *The Washington Post*, July 29, 2008.

23. "World Drug Report 2010," Vienna, Austria: UNODC, June 2010, p. 242.

24. The "2012 Failed States Index," Fund for Peace and Foreign Policy magazine, lists the following West Africa nations, along with their ranking (with "1" being the worst-failed state): Cote d'Ivoire (11), Guinea (12), Nigeria (14), Guinea-Bissau (15), Niger (18), Liberia (25), Sierra Leone (31), Mauritania (38), Togo (39), and Burkina Faso (41).

25. "UN says West Africa threatened by drug trafficking, organized crime," *Xinhua*, February 21, 2012.

26. Charlie Savage and Thom Shanker, "U.S. Drug War Expands to Africa, a Newer Hub for Cartels," *The New York Times*, July 21, 2012.

27. Ellis, abstract.

28. "Global Drug Trafficking: Africa's Expanding Role," Washington, DC: Woodrow Wilson International Center for Scholars: Africa Program, May 28, 2009, p. 5.

29. John Kelly, "Joint Regional Workshop on Harmonization of Drug Control Legislation in West Africa and Assessment of Dakar Initiative," Washington, DC: Africa Center for Strategic Studies (ACSS), September 2012.

30. Christophe Champin, "Les 'stups' français pessimistes sur le trafic de drogue en Afrique" ("French Anti-Drug Officials Pessimistic on Drug Trafficking in Africa"), RFI, Blog Afrique Drogue, March 11, 2012.

31. Ellis, p. 173.

32. Marina Reyskens/CAI, "Drug Economy: Africa and the international illicit drug trade," March 9, 2012, available from *DefenceWeb.com*.

33. Wyler and Cook, p. 1.

34. *Ibid.*, pp. 174-175.

35. *Ibid.*, p. 176.

36. Emmanuel Akyeampong, "Diaspora and Drug Trafficking in West Africa: A Case Study of Ghana," *African Affairs*, Vol. 104, No. 416, July 2005, pp. 431, 435-437, 443.

37. Wilson Center, p. 7.

38. Amado Philip de Andrés, "West Africa under Attack: Drugs, Organized Crime and Terrorism as the New Threats to Global Security," Madrid, Spain: Research Unit on International Security and Cooperation (UNISCI) Discussion Papers, No. 16, January 2008, p. 218.

39. *Ibid.*, p. 185.

40. Ellis, pp. 183-184.

41. Reyskens, 2012.

42. Christophe Champin, "Des policiers nigérians en pa-trouille en Suisse" ("Nigerian Policemen on Patrol in Switzerland"), RFI blogs, September 7, 2011.

43. Ellis, p. 184.

44. Christophe Champin, "Trafic des stupéfiants: le Nigeria renforce les contrôles sur les vols a destination de la Malaisie" ("Drug Trafficking: Nigeria Reinforces Controls on Flights Destined for Malaysia"), RFI blogs, December 27, 2011.

45. "West Africa–2012 ATS Situation Report," p. 19.

46. Interview with UNODC Representative for West Africa Alexander Schmidt, as reported in Christophe Champin, "Alexandre Schmidt: La capacité opérationnelle des narcotrafi-quants dépasse celle des Etats d'Afrique de l Ouest" ("Alexander Schmidt: The Operational Capacity of Narco-traffickers Exceeds

that of West African Nations"), RFI, Blog Afrique Drogue, June 29, 2011.

47. Ellis, p. 173.

48. Braun, p. 4.

49. Douglas Farah, "Transnational Drug Enterprises: Threats to Global Stability and U.S. National Security from Southwest Asia, Latin America and West Africa," testimony before House Committee on Oversight and Government Reform, October 1, 2009.

50. Douglas Farah, *Transnational Organized Crime, Terrorism, and Criminalized States in Latin America: An Emerging Tier-One National Security Priority*," Carlisle, PA: Strategic Studies Institute (SSI), U.S. Army War College, August 16, 2012, p. 27.

51. International Narcotics Control Strategy Report, Vol. 1, Drug and Chemical Control, Washington, DC: U.S. Department of State, Bureau for International Narcotics and Law Enforcement Affairs, March 2012, p. 230.

52. Akyeampong, p. 431.

53. Andrés, p. 205.

54. Paul Williams and Jurgen Haacke, "Security Culture, Transnational Challenges and the Economic Community of West African States," *Journal of Contemporary African Studies*, June 12, 2008.

55. *Ibid.*, p. 205.

56. Ellis, p. 185.

57. "West Africa - 2012 ATS Situation Report," p. 19.

58. Christophe Champin, "Trafic de drogue: l'Afrique de l'Ouest n'est ni la Colombie, ni le Mexique mais . . ." ("Drug Trafficking: West Africa is neither Colombia nor Mexico, but . . ."), RFI, Blog Afrique Drogue, June 3, 2011.

59. Christophe Champin, "Trafic de cocaïne: les Nigérians tissent leur toile en Italie dans l'ombre de la mafia" ("Cocaine Trafficking: Nigerians Weave their Web in Italy in the Shadow of the Mafia"), RFI, Blog Afrique Drogue, November 7, 2011.

60. Braun, p. 4.

61. Christophe Champin, "L'Afrique reste une plaque tournante pour l'héroïne, selon l'OICS" ("Africa Remains a Hub for Heroin, according to International Narcotics Control Board"), RFI, Blog Afrique Drogue, March 7, 2011.

62. Wilson Center, p. 8.

63. Harrigan, 2012, p. 1.

64. World Customs Office, as cited in Kelly, ACSS, September 2012.

65. William R. Brownfield, Written Statement, "Countering Narcotics Threats in West Africa," Washington, DC: Senate Caucus on International Narcotics Control, May 16, 2012, p. 2.

66. Harrigan, 2012, p. 8.

67. Thomas Harrigan, Statement before the U.S. Senate Committee on Foreign Relations Subcommittee on African Affairs, Washington, DC, June 23, 2009, available *from www.justice.gov/ola/...1/2009-06-23-dea-harrigan-west-africa.pdf.*

68. *Ibid.*, p. 11.

69. Alex Pena, "DEA: Mexican Drug Cartels Reach Further Across Africa," June 15, 2012, Voice of America (VOA).

70. "West Africa - 2012 ATS Situation Report," p. 12.

71. Champin, March 2, 2012.

72. "West Africa - 2012 ATS Situation Report," p. 9.

73. *Ibid.*, p. 11.

74. Christophe Champin, "Afrique, drogues synthétiques et marché des produits précurseurs" ("Africa, Synthetic Drugs and the Market for Precursor Products"), RFI, Blog Afrique Drogue, March 29, 2011.

75. Champin, March 3, 2011.

76. "West Africa - 2012 ATS Situation Report," p. 16.

77. October 25, 2010, available from *www.unodc.org/documents/ scientific/GSU4_FINAL_Web.pdf.*

78. "West Africa - 2012 ATS Situation Report," p. 20.

79. Deputy Assistant Secretary of Defense for Counternarcotics and Global Threats William Wechsler, Statement for the Record, "Countering Narcotics Threats in West Africa," Before the Senate Caucus on International Narcotics Control, May 16, 2012, p. 3.

80. "West Africa - 2012 ATS Situation Report," p. 21.

81. Christophe Champin, "Des réseaux Nigérians font du trafic de metamphétamines avec les yakuza" ("Nigerian Networks Traffic Methamphetamines with the Yakuza"), RFI, Blog Afrique Drogue, May 24, 2011.

82. Champin, February 27, 2012.

83. "West Africa - 2012 ATS Situation Report," p. 12.

84. International Narcotics Control Strategy Report, March 2012, p. 347.

85. "Amphetamines and Ecstasy: 2011 Global ATS Assessment," Vienna, Austria: UNODC, September 2011, p. 69.

86. Christophe Champin, "Nigéria: un nouveau laboratoire de drogues synthétiques démantèle" ("Nigeria: New Laboratory for Synthetic Drugs Dismantled"), RFI, Blog Afrique Drogue, February 27, 2012.

87. "West Africa Leaders Worried Over Drug Trafficking Situation," *Xinhua*, August 8, 2012.

88. Feinstein, 2012, p. 2-3.

89. Joint Regional Workshop, Senegal, April 2012.

90. Douglas Farah, Testimony on "Confronting Drug Trafficking in West Africa," Before The Senate Committee On Foreign Relations Subcommittee on African Affairs, June 23, 2009, p. 6.

91. Sebastian Rotella and Chris Kraul, "A drug's worrisome detour: Much of Europe's cocaine now arrives via West Africa, where the law means little," *Los Angeles Times*, March 14, 2007.

92. Wyler and Cook, p. 12.

93. Wyler and Cook, pp. 23-24.

94. "World Drug Report 2010," p. 242.

95. Wyler and Cook, p. 12.

96. *Ibid.*, p. 21.

97. Rotella and Kraul; 2007; UNODC 2007, p. 21.

98. Champin, March 11, 2012.

99. *Ibid.*, p. 10.

100. Wilson Center, p. 7.

101. "West Africa drugs trafficking 'increasingly sophisticated'," BBC NEWS: Africa, June 21, 2011.

102. Wyler and Cook, p. 11.

103. UNODC, 2007, p. 19.

104. Wilson Center, p. 7.

105. Champin, March 13, 2012.

106. Scott Baldauf, "Air Al Qaeda: Are Latin America's Drug Cartels Giving Al Qaeda a Lift?" *The Christian Science Monitor*, January 15, 2010.

107. Champin, March 13, 2012.

108. UNODC, 2007, p. 19.

109. Wyler and Cook, p. 13.

110. Christophe Champin, "L'intérêt des cartels de la cocaïne pour l'Afrique ne faiblit pas" ("Interest in Africa by Cocaine Cartels Does Not Weaken"), RFI, Blog Afrique Drogue, January 6, 2011.

111. Paul Melly, "Mayhem in Mali," *The World Today*, August/September 2012.

112. Farah, *Transnational Organized Crime*, p. 7.

113. Farah, Subcommittee on African Affairs, 2009, p. 6.

114. International Narcotics Control Strategy Report, March 2012, p. 241. Angola, another former Portuguese colony, is also an important transshipment point, according to this source.

115. Christophe Champin, "Drogue: les liaisons dangereuses entre le Brésil et l'Afrique" ("Drugs: Dangerous Liaisons Between Brazil and Africa"), RFI, Blog Afrique Drogue, November 17, 2011.

116. UNODC, 2007, p. 20.

117. David Blair, "Special Report: West Africa Welcomes Latin America's Drug Barons," *The Telegraph*, December 3, 2008.

118. Wyler and Cook, p. 13.

119. Abdelkader Abderrahmane, "Drug Trafficking and the Crisis in Mali," Pretoria, South Africa: Institute for Security Studies, August 6, 2012.

120. Harrigan, 2012, p. 7.

121. Ellis, p. 193, citing a January 4, 2008 BBC News Report, "Mali Cocaine Haul After Firefight."

122. International Narcotics Control Strategy Report, March 2012, p. 123.

123. UNODC, 2007, pp. 20-21.

124. William Wechsler, "Confronting Drug Trafficking in West Africa," Hearing before the Subcommittee on African Affairs, Committee on Foreign Relations, U.S. Senate, 111th Cong. 1st Sess., Washington, DC: U.S. Government Printing Office, June 23, 2009, p. 269, available from *allafrica.com/view/resource/main/ main/id/00011814.html*.

125. Antonio L. Mazzitelli, "Transnational Organized Crime in West Africa: The Additional Challenge," *International Affairs*, Vol. 83, No. 6, 2007.

126. Farah, Subcommittee on African Affairs, 2009.

127. *Ibid.*, pp. 4, 7; DEA Congressional Testimony 2010; Farah, House Committee on Oversight and Government Reform, October 1, 2009.

128. Wechsler, 2012, pp. 1-2.

129. *Ibid.*

130. Baldauf, 2010.

131. Farah, Subcommittee on African Affairs, 2009, p. 5.

132. Ellis, p. 192.

133. Christophe Champin, "Un important réseau de narco trafics démantelé enter les Etats-Unis et le Liberia" (An Impor-

tant Network of Drug Traffickers Dismantled Between the United States and Liberia"), RFI, Blog Afrique Drogue, June 3, 2011.

134. Harrigan, 2012, p. 9.

135. UN Secretary-General Ban Ki-Moon, in remarks to the Security Council meeting on the impact of transnational organized crime on peace, security, and stability in West Africa and the Sahel, in New York, February 21, 2012.

136. John Campbell, "Will the Radical Islam Shoe Drop in West Africa?" Washington, DC: Council on Foreign Relations, September 18, 2012.

137. Harrigan, 2012, p. 9.

138. Felbab-Brown, pp. 6-7.

139. Comments of an anonymous subject-matter expert who spoke with the author on May 15, 2012. In his June 29, 2011, interview with RFI, UNODC West Africa Representative Schmidt also felt that terrorist elements in the Sahel-Sahara charged a "service fee" to allow illicit trafficking of drugs, cigarettes, arms, medicines, and people, but was not ready at that point to say that terrorist groups in the Sahel-Sahara were directly involved in the drug trade.

140. "World Drug Report 2010," p. 244.

141. Farah, Subcommittee on African Affairs, 2009, p. 8.

142. Ellis, p. 193.

143. Christophe Champin, "Un vaste réseau libanais de trafic de drogue et de blanchiment avec des ramifications en Afrique dans le collimateur des Etats-Unis" ("A Vast Lebanese Network for Drug Trafficking and Money Laundering with Ramifications for Africa in the Crosshairs of the United States"), RFI blogs, January 28, 2011.

144. DEA Congressional Testimony, 2010.

145. Farah, Subcommittee on African Affairs, 2009, p. 8.

146. Wechsler, 2012, p. 4.

147. *The New York Times*, December 2011, as cited in John Kelly, ACSS, "Joint Regional Workshop on Harmonization of Drug Control Legislation in West Africa and Assessment of Dakar Initiative," September 2012.

148. Christophe Champin, "Blanchiment d'argent de la drogue: guerre de communiques entre la DEA américaine et une banque libanaise" ("Laundering of Drug Money: War of Press Releases Between the U.S. DEA and a Lebanese Bank"), RFI blogs, February 28, 2011.

149. Grassley, May 16, 2012, p. 2.

150. Harrigan, 2012, p. 7.

151. UN Secretary-General Ban Ki-Moon, New York, February 21, 2012.

152. Reyskens, 2012.

153. Wyler and Cook, p. 7.

154. "Drug Trafficking as a Security Threat in West Africa," New York: UN Office on Drugs and Crime, October 2008.

155. "World Drug Report 2010," p. 245.

156. Christophe Champin, "Ahemdou Ould Abdallah: Beaucoup de dirigeants sont connectés au trafic de drogue en Afrique de l'Ouest" ("Ahemdou Ould Abdallah: Many Leaders are Connected to the Drug Trade in West Africa"), interview with Christophe Champin, RFI blogs, February 3, 2012.

157. Davin O'Regan, "Narco-States: Africa's Next Menace," *The New York Times*, March 13, 2012.

158. Wilson Center, p. 15.

159. Christophe Champin, "Réunion confidentielle entre le président ghanéens et les officiers de liaison anti-drogue occidentaux" ("Confidential Meeting Between Ghana President and Western Anti-Drug Liaison Officers"), RFI, Blog Afrique Drogue, February 1, 2011.

160. Conversation between the author and an anonymous subject-matter expert, May 8, 2012.

161. "World Drug Report 2010," p. 244.

162. The Minister was rehired, per an anonymous subject-matter expert, conversation with author, May 15, 2012.

163. Mazzitelli, 2007.

164. James Cockayne, "Africa and the War on Drugs: The West African Cocaine Trade is Not Just Business as Usual," *African Arguments*, October 19, 2012; Neil Carrier and Gernot Kantschnig, commenting on "Africa and the War on Drugs," *African Arguments*, October 2012.

165. Anonymous subject-matter expert, February 17, 2012.

166. Felbab-Brown, p. 2.

167. *Ibid.*, p. 3.

168. "World Drug Report 2010," p. 242.

169. Felbab-Brown, p. 3.

170. *Ibid.*, p. 3.

171. Champin, June 29, 2011.

172. Christophe Champin, "Mauritanie: un trafiquant de drogue français en cavale" ("Mauritania: a French Drug Trafficker On the Run"), RFI blogs, September 13, 2011.

173. Wilson Center, p. 13.

174. Felbab-Brown, p. 1-2.

175. Farah, Subcommittee on African Affairs, 2009, p. 4.

176. Based on the author's May 8, 2012, conversation with anonymous subject-matter expert.

177. Ellis, p. 172; Reyskens, 2012.

178. Champin, June 3, 2011.

179. Cockayne, October 2012.

180. Farah, *Transnational Organized Crime, Terrorism, and Criminalized States in Latin America*, p. 30.

181. International Narcotics Control Strategy Report, March 2012, p. 232.

182. UNODC, 2007, p. 30.

183. Felbab-Brown, p. 6.

184. Conversation between the author and an anonymous subject-matter expert, May 15, 2012.

185. *Ibid.*, p. 6.

186. Some observers note that Guinea-Bissau had very little state capacity to begin with and opine that being "captured" begs the question: Why does that matter? One such observer asserts that what has been captured in Guinea-Bissau are the organs of the state, i.e., military, law enforcement sectors, etc., with agents of the state now working as agents of the DTOs. Since the government never actually delivered rule of law, security, or public services to the population, this shift has not fundamentally altered how the "social contract" works in Guinea-Bissau.

187. Wechsler, 2009, p. 2.

188. O'Regan.

189. *Ibid.*, p. 241.

190. Christophe Champin, "International Crisis Group s'interroge sur la poursuite du trafic de cocaïne en Guinee-Bissau" ("International Crisis Group Questions the Pursuit of Cocaine Trafficking in Guinea-Bissau"), RFI, Glog Afrique Drogue, January 24, 2012.

191. Champin, March 11, 2012.

192. Conversation with an anonymous subject-matter expert, May 8, 2012. Generational tensions are a historical feature of the military in Guinea-Bissau that pre-exist the drug trade. The country writ large in fact has been described as a "gerontocracy," but nowhere is this as evident as in the military. Drug revenues have exacerbated this trend.

193. Ashley Bybee, *Narco-State or Failed State: Politics and Narcotics in Guinea-Bissau,* Unpublished Ph.D. dissertation, George Mason University, School of Public Policy, 2012.

194. UNODC has also supported TCUs in Liberia and Sierra Leone.

195. UNODC Executive Director Yury Fedotov, "Guinea-Bissau's leaders address concerns about drug trafficking in West Africa," UN Press release, October 27, 2011.

196. Carson, pp. 6-7.

197. International Narcotics Control Strategy Report, March 2012, p. 242.

198. *Ibid.*

199. Ellis, p. 172.

200. Wechsler, 2012, p. 5.

201. *Ibid.*, p. 3.

202. Farah, Subcommittee on African Affairs, 2009.

203. UNODC Executive Director, October 27, 2011.

204. *Xinhua*, February 21, 2012.

205. Joint Regional Workshop on Harmonization of Drug Control Legislation, Senegal, April 2012.

206. Champin, June 29, 2011.

207. Wilson Center, p. 10.

208. Christophe Champin, "L'Afrique, plaque tournante et terre de consommation de l'héroïne afghane" ("Africa, Trafficking Hub and Land of Consumption of Afghan Heroin"), RFI, Africa drug blog, January 18, 2012.

209. International Narcotics Control Strategy Report, March 2012, p. 230.

210. "West Africa – 2012 ATS Situation Report," pp. 19, 29.

211. Comments by Ghanaian subject-matter expert to author, February 17, 2012.

212. *Ibid.*, p. 231.

213. An anonymous subject-matter expert estimated the number of heroin addicts in Nigeria to be as large as 500,000 to 600,000, based in part on a similar addiction problem in Kenya. However, another source indicated that UNODC had estimated that there were 1.2 million heroin addicts in all of Africa, which suggests that this Nigeria estimate is inflated.

214. Interview with author, May 15, 2012.

215. Wilson Center, p. 9.

216. Ashley Neese Bybee, "Narco-State or Failed State? Narcotics and Politics in Guinea-Bissau," Alexandria, VA: Institute for Defense Analyses, September 2011, p. 6.

217. Carson.

218. Anonymous Ghana subject-matter expert, February 17, 2012.

219. Costa.

220. Dr. Abdullahi Shehu, Director General of the Inter-Governmental Action Group Against Money Laundering in West Africa (GIABA), "Drug Trafficking and its Impact on West Africa," paper presented at meeting of the Joint Committee on Political Affairs, Peace and Security/ New Partnership for Africa's Development (NEPAD) and Africa Peer Review Mechanism of the ECOWAS Parliament, Katsina, Nigeria, July 28-August 1, 2009, p. 1.

221. Reyskens, 2012.

222. Conversation with anonymous subject-matter expert, May 8, 2012.

223. Ellis, p. 189.

224 . Costa.

225. Ellis, p. 178.

226. Felbab-Brown, p. 4.

227. Anonymous Ghana subject-matter expert, February 17, 2012.

228. Ellis, p. 178.

229. Mazzitelli, 2007.

230. Reyskens, 2010.

231. O'Regan, 2012.

232. Farah, Subcommittee on African Affairs, 2009, p. 2

233. Danielle Kurtzleben, "Africa-US: Growing Drug Trade Linked to Terror Groups," Inter Press Service, 2009.

234. Grassley, p. 2-3.

235. Wilson Center, p. 13.

236. *Ibid.*

237. As quoted from UNISI Discussion Paper No. 16, January 2008, available from *www.ucm.es/info/unisci/revistas/ UNISCI_DP_16_-_Andres.pdf.*

238. *Ibid.*

239. *Ibid.,* p. 26.

240. Christophe Champin, "Cocaïne, latinos et truands hollandaise en Gambie" ("Cocaine, Latinos, and Dutch Thugs in Gambia"), RFI, Blog Afrique Drogue, October 21, 2011.

241. Carson.

242. Shehu, pp. 5-6.

243. Carson.

244. Reyskens, 2012.

245. UNSC S/2012/45, Letter dated January 18, 2012, from the Secretary-General addressed to the President of the Security Council, available from *undocs.org/S/2012/45.*

246. Based on the author's May 8, 2012, conversation with an anonymous subject-matter expert.

247. Wechsler, 2009, p. 3.

248. Carson.

249. International Narcotics Control Strategy Report, 2012, p. 347.

250. ECOWAS Ministerial Conference on Drug Trafficking as a Security Threat to West Africa, Republic of Cape Verde, October 28, 2008, *available from www.un.org/sg/statements/index. asp?nid=3503.*

251. "EU-INTERPOL symposium provides forum for enhanced international police cooperation against transnational crime in West Africa," INTERPOL, September 30, 2010, Press Release.

252. "Customs and Police Target Drug Couriers in Operations at Airports Across Africa and Brazil," INTERPOL, February 13, 2012, Press Release.

253. Savage and Shanker.

254. *Ibid.*

255. WACSI was launched at a USG-EU co-hosted Transatlantic Symposium on Drug Trafficking in Portugal in May 2011.

256. Wechsler, 2012, p. 4.

257. *Ibid.*

258. Brownfield, 2012, p. 6.

259. Savage and Shanker.

260. The other African countries where the DEA currently has offices are Egypt, Kenya, and South Africa.

261. Harrigan, 2012, p. 4, 7.

262. *Ibid.*, p. 4. The DEA will also establish in 2012 an SIU in Nairobi, Kenya.

263. Braun, p. 7.

264. Carson.

265. Bybee, p. 6.

266. Wechsler, 2009, p. 3.

267. Wechsler, 2012, p. 4.

268. Nicole Dalrymple, "AFRICOM-funded Projects Assisting African Partners Develop Capacity to Counter Drug Trafficking," USAFRICOM Public Affairs, January 6, 2012.

269. International Narcotics Control Strategy Report, 2012, p. 232.

270. Wechsler, 2009, pp. 3-4.

271. *Ibid.*, p. 4.

272. International Narcotics Control Strategy Report, 2012, p. 232.

273. Wechsler, 2009, p. 1.

274. Wyler, 2009.

275. Jim Lobe, "U.S.-West Africa: Report Urges Enhanced Maritime Security," Inter Press Service, December 6, 2010.

276. Felbab-Brown, p. 7.

277. Feinstein, pp. 2-3.

278. As paraphrased from Costa.

279. UNODC, 2007, p. 33.

280. *Ibid.*, p. 1.

281. O'Regan, 2012.

282. Shehu, p. 12.

283. The "Dakar Initiative Against Drugs," available from *www.dakarcontreladrogue.com/Home/tabid/122/language/en-US/Default.aspx.*

284. Remarks by U.S. Ambassador to Senegal and Guinea-Bissau Lewis Lukens, Counter-narcotics Harmonization Inter-Ministerial Conference, September 12, 2012, Dakar.